Early explorations in science

Exploring Primary Science and Technology

Series Editor: Brian Woolnough
Department of Educational Studies, University of Oxford

Science is one of the most exciting and challenging subjects within the National Curriculum. This innovative new series is designed to help primary school teachers to cope with the curriculum demands by offering a range of stimulating and accessible texts grounded in the very best of primary practice. Each book is written by an experienced practitioner and seeks to inspire and encourage whilst at the same time acknowledging the realities of classroom life.

Current and forthcoming titles

Jenny Frost: *Creativity in primary science*
Jane Johnston: *Early explorations in science*
Anne Quatter: *Differentiated primary science*

Early explorations in science

JANE JOHNSTON

OPEN UNIVERSITY PRESS
Buckingham • *Philadelphia*

Open University Press
Celtic Court
22 Ballmoor
Buckingham
MK18 1XW

and
1900 Frost Road, Suite 101
Bristol, PA 19007, USA

First Published 1996

A catalogue record of this book is available from the British Library

ISBN 0 335 19540 7 (pb)   0 335 19541 5 (hb)

Library of Congress Cataloging-in-Publication Data
Johnston, Jane, 1954–
    Early explorations in science / Jane Johnston.
        p. cm.
    Includes bibliographical references and index.
    ISBN 0–335–19540–7 (pbk.). — ISBN 0–335–19541–5
    1. Science—Study and teaching (Preschool).   I. Title.
LB1140.5.S36J64   1996
372.3—dc20   95–44210
                                                                     CIP

Typeset by Graphicraft Typesetters Limited, Hong Kong
Printed in Great Britain by St Edmundsbury Press,
Bury St Edmunds, Suffolk

Contents

List of figures and tables

Series editor's preface

One of the great achievements in the educational system of England and Wales over the last decade has been the growth of science and technology teaching in the primary school. Previously this had been weak and spasmodic, often centring on the nature table and craft work; now it is well established in the curriculum of all children from the age of 5. Primary school teachers are to be congratulated on this achievement, building their science work on often uncertain foundations. This is therefore an appropriate time for this series of books which looks in detail at what has been achieved, and seeks to develop the fundamental principles that underlie the ways in which children learn and teachers teach science and technology in primary schools.

Two approaches to primary school science had been developing prior to the introduction of a National Curriculum. The first saw investigations as the focus of the children's work, studying aspects of their natural environment to develop both an insight into the underlying science and the way that scientists work. The second approach was modelled more on the way in which science had been taught in the secondary school and centred on the content of science which needed to be taught. When the National Curriculum for science was introduced in 1989 it sought, not entirely satisfactorily, to bring together these two approaches, with half the curriculum being given to explorations and investigations and half to the content of science. In this series we are seeking to explore primary science and technology further. We perceive science and technology as more than an accretion of skills and knowledge but rather as a holistic activity involving pupils' hands, minds and hearts. For the pupils to fully learn and appreciate science and technology they will need to develop their attitudes, experiences and knowledge through activities which challenge and stimulate them, and in which they find success and satisfaction. We seek both to educate children *in* science and technology and *through* science and technology, helping them both to appreciate and enjoy these subjects and through them to develop their personality and sense of self worth.

Doing science and technology is a very personal and individualistic matter. Learning science, like the learning of everything else of real worth, is a messy, unpredictable but ultimately satisfying process. One of the benefits of a National Curriculum is that it establishes the place of science and technology in the curriculum. One of the great weaknesses of the English National Curriculum is that it has prescribed the content around an assessment structure which infers linear progression foreign to the way children really learn. Children learn (differentially according to their aptitudes and strengths) by personal exploration; by testing out their ideas in discussion and writing; by being encouraged when they are on the right lines, and corrected when they seem to be heading off in the wrong direction and are using the language of science inappropriately. The teacher's vital and sensitive task is to provide the appropriate stimulation in scientific and technological contexts, to allow the children to express their thinking, and to encourage and correct them as appropriate. In such a way children will construct their own understanding and attitudes to science and technology and become members of the broader scientific and technological community.

Jane Johnston's book brings a wealth of experience and insight into the area of childrens early explorations in science. She encourages us to build on the very real experiences of science that the children have before commencing school and which they bring with them into their earliest 'science lessons'. She stresses the importance of individual explorations in the development of science knowledge and skills in the early years and the need to seek creativity in science activities. Overall, she shows how the teachers role can blend the apparently impossible demands provided by each individual child with the realistic possibility of working with a whole class in normal situations. She blends both practical experience and perceptive insight in a way which only a genuinely empathetic and inspirational teacher can. This book will make an important contribution in developing and establishing the teaching of science in the early years.

Acknowledgements

I would like to acknowledge the help and support of the following people in writing this book:

- the staff and children of Butler's Hill Infant and Nursery School, Hucknall, for their help and cooperation;
- students (past and present) from the Department of Primary Education, Nottingham Trent University, for providing me with thoughtful observations of teaching and learning;
- Jim Johnson, for his help with my writing;
- Brian Woolnough, for his constructive comments and enthusiasm;
- Chris, Emily and Andrew, for their help, hindrance and encouragement.

1

Pre-school science experiences

Pre-school science experiences are diverse and numerous; before children arrive in school they experience science in all aspects of their lives. As teachers, we need to be aware of these experiences and their importance in subsequent school development in order effectively to develop scientific ideas, skills and attitudes in the children we teach. It is helpful not only to have an awareness of the types of experience children have, but also to have a clear idea about the nature of our own science experiences. These experiences have helped make us who we are and are important in understanding our own perspective on science. For example, I can remember positive science experiences before and during primary school which have helped to make me feel positive towards science and assisted my early scientific understanding. I have, however, my fair share of horror stories about later science experiences which not only tempered my enthusiasm for a while, but also hindered my development, particularly in physical sciences.

Additional important understanding comes from knowledge

of the history and philosophy of science. This is not only of great interest but also of great importance in understanding the relevance of science to individuals and to society. Questions such as 'What were the major influential scientific discoveries?', 'Who made these discoveries?' and 'How have these discoveries affected my everyday life?' are important to ask and to answer. This knowledge is necessary in addition to understanding the diversity of ideas which make up science, as well as understanding the ideas themselves. In short, we need to know about children, about science knowledge and about the nature of science.

Throughout this book the phrase 'the nature of science' refers to the science relevant to young children, and in this introductory chapter I am referring to the science of life from an under-fives perspective. It should be noted that a wider understanding is essential to enable us effectively to facilitate scientific development in young children.

What is science?

This question is an extremely difficult one to answer accurately, because the subject is as vast as the universe and can be perceived in numerous different ways. Our understanding of science is shaped by our experiences, and these in turn are influenced by our educational system and society. Differences in society and educational emphasis have been found (Hayes and Johnston, 1993; 1995) to affect views of science. In Finland primary science has a biological and geographical emphasis, and Finnish society places special importance on the environment and environmental education. As a result, Finnish primary teachers will describe science using words such as 'nature', 'living', 'organisms', 'pollution', 'environment' and 'ecology'. For primary teachers in England and Wales, on the other hand, science, in the main, is described in terms of the scientific process, with words such as 'experimenting', 'investigating' and 'finding out'. They appear to interpret the question 'What do you think science involves?' as 'What do you think school/primary science involves?', reflecting the influence of their most recent and significant experiences. They have been influenced by the emphasis placed on the process of science in primary science teaching and learning. In a similar way, the experiences of school science feature in many minds when the word 'science' is uttered (Johnston, 1995), because school science is the most significant science experience in most people's lives. Adults have a variety of science experiences and a broader understanding of science than children. However, they often do not have a full understanding of the breadth of science applications or the extensive nature of science.

Science is also commonly described as a 'body of knowledge' or a 'body of facts' associated with particular disciplines such as biology, physics, chemistry, geology, astronomy, psychology, computing technology, and so on. Underlying these descriptions of science is the assumption that scientific knowledge is certain and unchanging. In reality, of course, we cannot be certain about knowledge and must acknowledge its provisional nature. New discoveries broaden our understanding of the universe, changing the way we think and the way we view the world. In this way, science is better described as a body of theories, with the present theories being tentative in nature and being replaced with new and better theories as our understanding grows. The provisional knowledge which is science is embedded in general notions or concepts associated with the wide-ranging disciplines. Education in England and Wales has identified certain concepts and knowledge which are associated with science (Department for Education, 1995a). These can be seen in Table 1.1. The concept of plant growth would be embedded in the discipline of biology or Attainment Target 2, 'Life Processes and Living Things'. The knowledge within that concept appropriate for young children would include the requirements for plant growth, how a plant grows and different methods of seed dispersal. The concept of force would be embedded in the discipline of physics or Attainment Target 4, 'Physical Processes', and would involve knowledge about different types of forces and their effects (moving, slowing, accelerating, changing). As children develop physically and intellectually, so does their understanding of scientific concepts and their knowledge becomes deeper and broader.

Like scientific concepts and knowledge, scientific skills also develop in breadth and depth. Scientific skills are essentially those skills developed during the scientific process and employed to a greater or lesser extent in our everyday lives. We observe the world around us and begin to ask questions about what we see. We group things together (classify) and identify similarities and differences. We make plans, investigate, predict and hypothesize.

Table 1.1   Science at Key Stage 1 of the National Curriculum, 1995

Attainment Target 1: Experimental and investigative science
• Planning experimental procedures
• Obtaining evidence
• Considering evidence

Attainment Target 2: Life processes and living things
• Life processes
• Humans as organisms
• Green plants as organisms
• Variation and classification
• Living·things in their environment

Attainment Target 3: Materials and their properties
• Grouping materials
• Changing materials

Attainment Target 4: Physical processes
• Electricity
• Forces and motion
• Light and sound

Source: Department for Education (1995a).

We measure, record, interpret and communicate. If we are buying a new car we look closely at a number of models and compare their features and functions. We test-drive cars, perhaps making notes about each one according to the main criteria we have decided upon. Interpretation and reflection allow us to make informed decisions about each car and our final decision is based upon knowledge gained through the use of scientific skills. A number of the scientific skills are encompassed by exploration and these are described in more detail in Chapter 2.

Scientific attitudes are equal in importance to concepts, knowledge and skills. They fall into two categories: attitudes *to* science and attitudes *in* science. Attitudes in science can be further divided into attitudes involved with motivation, investigation, group participation and reflection. Our success or failure in any scientific endeavour is closely associated with our attitudes to and in science and will in turn affect the development of those same attitudes. These are considered in more detail in Chapter 4.

The scientific concepts, knowledge, skills and attitudes which young children are developing concern their everyday lives and the world around them. Science is not concerned with laboratories, test-tubes and Bunsen burners, but with real life. It is real science, relevant science, albeit in many cases unsophisticated, undeveloped or even not obviously science (tacit science). Children should be developing scientific concepts, knowledge, skills and attitudes equally. It is important that they form good foundations for future conceptual understanding and do not develop misconceptions, but it is equally important that they develop skills which will be of general use in their future lives, in and out of school, and that they develop positive attitudes to and in science. Without positive attitudes, conceptual and skill development will be impaired, and without scientific skills both future conceptual development and everyday life skills will be hampered.

The informal development of scientific ideas, skills and attitudes

From the moment of birth, or even from the moment of conception, children are developing scientific ideas about the world around them. These ideas occur as a result of experiences and exploration. Scientific conceptual development begins at an early age, earlier than many people would have thought possible. In the womb the foetus is able to make use of many senses, recognizing and being comforted by a variety of sounds. A baby soon learns to recognize voices, music and other familiar sounds and will turn its head towards its mother's voice or settle to a familiar melody.

As they grow, babies learn quickly about the existence of gravity, as they drop things out of their prams or high chairs. It becomes a game to throw away your toys and wait for someone else to rescue them. These young children know exactly where to look for discarded toys: they look down. They have learnt the rule that when you drop things they fall. At bath time the concept of forces is established further through exploration of floating and sinking. Bath toys can be pushed under the water and some will bob back up, while others will sink. Other toys can be made to sink by filling with water. Children spend countless hours filling containers and emptying them, siphoning water through tubes, splashing and 'swimming' in the bath. Bath time is a wonderful opportunity to explore many scientific phenomena in an everyday setting. Bubble bath, shampoo and soap all provide opportunities to explore materials. A bar of soap can be explored in a number of ways, squashing, making bubbles, soap shapes or mixing soap and water. Thus playing in the bath is quite likely to result in a liquid soap mess, but will also lead to some understanding of the nature of materials and what happens when you mix them.

Early meals will also establish ideas about the nature of different materials, the mixing of materials and how those materials change. Children soon learn that rusks are hard but ease growing teeth, whereas liquidized food is sloppy and soft. When food is given separately it is great fun to mix it all together to form a messy mass, even if you are not going to eat it. Spoons make nice noises on the table and attract attention, and drinks will spill out if held upside down, even in teacher beakers.

Children's toys will help to establish ideas and skills in science. Children will explore their toys, or even the boxes they come in! They learn to look closely at the toys and explore how they work. They will often find new and novel ways of playing with their toys, but all are valid and will help to develop their ideas and skills. Mechanical, electrical and magnetic toys begin to develop ideas about energy and movement, as well as other types of energy such as light, sound and electricity. Noisy and musical toys develop ideas about sound. Construction toys develop ideas about structures and forces. Cycles, swings, climbing frames and other large toys develop knowledge about balance and movement. Through all the normal exploration of childhood, children will be developing many scientific concepts, but they will also be developing scientific skills. Hand–eye coordination, fine motor skills, observational skills, classification skills and prediction skills will be of use in later scientific development.

Walks in the woods, or in the local park, visits to adventure playgrounds and interactive museums, bus and train journeys and holidays will all add to these experiences and widen the developing ideas, skills and attitudes. Children will learn about the seasons, flowers, animals, trees, the weather and much more. The birth of new brothers, sisters, cousins or friends will provide knowledge of pregnancy, birth and growth. Personal hygiene and cleanliness, sickness and daily routine will help to develop skills and knowledge which will be of use in later life.

Throughout the early years of life scientific concepts, knowledge and skills are being developed through exploration of the

Figure 1.1 Factors affecting the quality of early explorations

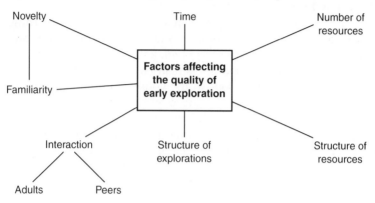

child's world. There are a number of factors which will affect the quality of early years explorations, and these are described in Figure 1.1.

The more exploratory experiences children have, the greater their scientific development is likely to be. Providing a variety of different exploratory play resources will assist this development. Children should be encouraged to explore as many diverse resources as possible and should only be restricted by a concern for safety and consideration of other living things. Care should be taken that gender bias is not exercised, even unintentionally, and it is important not to discourage children in their experiences. Children who are discouraged from construction toys will be denied important manipulative and structural experiences; as children discouraged from 'dressing up' will have fewer opportunities to explore different textiles and their properties.

It is also important to provide ample time for exploration to occur. Children need time for free exploration and should not be rushed from one experience to another. We all value a period of quiet contemplation in our lives, and children are no exception. If we rush them from one experience to another they will have little opportunity to try out their developing ideas and build upon existing ideas. At this young age much learning occurs through trial and error, and this takes time and patience. Strangely enough, children appear to have more patience at this age than we give them credit for and will explore a simple toy for a considerable length of time. As children develop, their interest appears to be held for shorter periods of time, perhaps because we teach them to 'value' time!

Children will benefit from both new experiences and returning to old ones. They need to return to familiar play resources and see different ways of exploring them, and this sometimes occurs best if access to play resources is restricted. Toys put away for a few weeks are like new toys to the young child and can stimulate new exploration. Structuring playtime can help to prevent children from sensory overload through having too many toys or play resources, or from moving quickly from one activity to another. If children are used to having all their toys out at the beginning of every day then they will quickly become bored with them. If different combinations of toys are provided they may find new and novel ways of exploring them.

A final factor affecting the quality of exploration is the amount of interaction during exploratory play. At this stage of development, the most important interaction occurs with adults. Too little interaction and the children may lack motivation and lose interest quickly. Too much adult involvement and the exploration may be too structured, the children may become too dependent on adult help and opportunities may not be provided for free exploration. Through these explorations, children will also be developing useful scientific attitudes. Their explorations can encourage them to be curious and inventive and begin to ask questions about their world.

Children are constantly learning about the world around them and the scientific concepts they meet and develop are relevant to their world. Pre-school children will have some very firm ideas about the world around them. These ideas are the result of a whole range of experiences, and even though they are sometimes limited they can be wide ranging and diverse. When they enter more formal education these explorations and the ideas developed as a result will have an important influence on their subsequent development. Children do not start school devoid of scientific ideas. No one is completely ignorant of science, but some of these early scientific experiences will be of more benefit than others. Children who have had considerable pre-school experiences will benefit in many ways. My own classroom experiences have indicated that children who have stimulating pre-school experiences such as good parental/home interaction, play group and nursery experiences, are likely to be advantaged. In addition, the children's birthdays and schools' admissions policies mean that some children have additional Key Stage 1 experiences. In the UK children born between 1 September and 31 August of the following year will be in the same academic year and will move through the key stages together. However, school admissions policies differ. All children should begin their period of compulsory schooling by the beginning of the term after which they are five years of age, but they may begin earlier. Some children will begin school at the beginning of the academic year in which they are five years of age, others the term before their birthday and others the day after their birthday. In addition to the differences in school admissions policies and the subsequent length of time they are taught within Key Stage 1, there may be differences in both maturation and pre-school experiences. Children will develop differently and at different rates. They will have different experiences and respond differently to them. The result of these differences is a wide mix of abilities and experiences within even our first classroom, making the role of the teacher more challenging. For example, children born on 1 September may have stimulating pre-school (home and playgroup experiences) until they are three years old. They may have nursery education from three years of age and enter school at the beginning of the academic year in which they are five years of age, when the class size is small. These children will therefore spend three terms as reception infants before moving into Year 1. Other children may be born on 31 August of the following year but be in the same academic year. They may have poor pre-school experiences, and no nursery education. They could begin school the term after their fifth birthday, immediately entering Year 1 with older children who have had reception experience. At the end of Key Stage 1 the result is that some children entering Key Stage 2 have seven full years of stimulating experiences to reflect on, while others have only two years at Key Stage 1 to enhance their development. As educators we can ensure that the two or three years at Key Stage 1 are stimulating and we can provide opportunities for quality exploration, but we have no control over the pre-school experiences of the children we teach. As a result, children entering school at five years of age have diverse needs and abilities.

Let us look briefly at the role of parents in providing pre-school exploratory experiences. Very few parents set out with the intention of harming their children's development. Most want to provide experiences which will help their children's development in school and beyond. Many are not informed about the benefits of different experiences for different skills and conceptual development. If parents are not aware of the benefits of experiences which can develop fine motor skills, spatial awareness, observational skills, personal skills and conceptual development, they will be unable to provide the best opportunities for their children. Being a parent is one of the most difficult jobs in the world and it is the job we are often least prepared for. We should not assume that all parents are aware of the need to provide different experiences for their children any more than we should assume that they are aware of details about birth and pregnancy. Our society provides support during pregnancy, birth and early life and then only interferes if we make a complete muddle of child-rearing. I met one small child in her first year of life who was unable to play with toys, had difficulties feeding and would not handle her food. Her carers knew nothing of the benefits of talking to her and giving her opportunities to handle food and toys, to put things into her mouth and explore what they feel, taste or smell like. When she smiled it was rare and the first 'raspberry' she blew was a milestone. Even at this young age it took considerable efforts to begin to provide the missed opportunities and make up for the lack of early development.

The experiences of young children may contain abstract ideas about a wide range of scientific phenomena, but the scientific knowledge being developed by the young children will be the result of concrete experiences. In many instances young children will be developing knowledge about scientific phenomena but unaware of its scientific nature. At a later stage of development we will be able to focus attention on the ideas developing from these early experiences and guide understanding. However, we should remember that full understanding of any phenomena is a long-term goal.

More formal development of scientific ideas and skills and attitudes

When children mix in more formal ways with other children and adults, in mother and toddler groups, playgroups and nurseries, they develop additional skills and build upon the knowledge they have already developed. They also begin to learn to work with others, to cooperate and to share ideas and skills. These life skills are essential to more formal learning, and children who have not begun to develop them by the time they enter school at five may find school an alien environment. If the first few months of formal schooling are spent learning social skills, then the development of concepts, knowledge, skills and attitudes is likely to be affected. Playgroups and nursery education should provide a progression in the development of exploration, both widening experiences and deepening them and are therefore an important stepping-stone to Key Stage 1 education.

In the nursery or playgroup, children have opportunities to work collaboratively in a variety of exploratory play situations. Explorations of materials can occur using everyday nursery play resources. Finger painting and play dough can provide opportunities for children to explore materials using their senses. Cornflour and water mixed provides a lovely medium for using senses and language development. The addition of food colouring can add to the fun. I have used cornflour and water mix, more formally, to help children with shape or letter formation. It is much more fun than writing or drawing and just as beneficial. Sand and water play can have many scientific dimensions. Wet sand and dry sand can be compared for their building qualities. Coloured water or water of different temperatures can be used.

Nursery pets can provide opportunities to observe living things and to care for them. Birthdays, new births and starting school can all provide opportunities to develop ideas about human growth and life cycles. Seasonal weather and its effect on plant and animal life can all provide additional opportunities to consider growth in the environment. The opportunities are seemingly endless.

Other play resources will develop ideas about forces. Construction toys can be used to explore how tall a structure can be made. Cycles and other moving toys can be pushed and pulled. Water play can involve development of ideas about floating and sinking. During these explorations the interaction of the carer is important. A questioning approach can help children to develop their ideas, for example 'How can we sink this boat?'

Occasional activities can add to everyday science in the classroom. The provision of ice balloons can provoke wonder and provide additional opportunities to explore. I have used ice balloons in explorations with children of a wide range of ages and in a variety of situations. Ice balloons were described by Ovens (1987) and later used in exploratory situations (Lewis, 1992). An ice balloon is made by carefully filling a balloon with water from a tap. I stress the word 'carefully', as experience has shown me that if the balloon comes off the tap, you and the room get very wet! The resulting balloon looks similar to a water bomb. It can be placed in a freezer and left for a few days to freeze solid. It is better if you put it into a plastic container in the freezer, because if it bursts it does make quite a mess. You can use a variety of different shaped balloons or even try other containers. I have tried a rubber glove and it was received with great interest, although the fingers melt quite quickly. Using food colouring or paint to colour the water adds another dimension to the ice balloon explorations. Having already suggested leaving the balloon to freeze solid, a half-frozen balloon can make an interesting comparison and lead to exploration as to how the water freezes and water crystals are formed. Explorations such as these can aid the development of a number of scientific concepts and skills which are described further in Chapter 2.

Nursery exploration in action

I put two ice balloons on the table in a school nursery and allowed the children freely to explore. The balloons created a great deal of enthusiasm and it was interesting to note that they did not ask 'What does it do?' or 'What does it make?', as children often do when given new resources. First the children looked at them. Some children immediately touched the balloons, while others were more reserved and would not touch them until they had looked at them for some time. They then pushed them around the table and were surprised because they were slippery. One child noticed the rubber of the balloon had broken and was peeling away a little. She was amazed that there was ice inside the balloon.

Ice!
It's cold!
Freezing!

Then the children peeled the balloons and looked again. They tried sliding one balloon across the table and had great fun exploring its slippery qualities again. They noted that it was easier to slide without the rubber, but offered no explanation of why this was so. Meanwhile the remaining balloon had stuck fast to the table. One child was convinced that this was because it had a small piece of rubber underneath it. He put another piece of rubber under it but it did not stick, partly because he did not leave it for any length of time! However, he was still convinced that the rubber made it stick. The first balloon remained stuck to the table for some time and took considerable efforts to remove so other explorations could continue! After a period of further exploration and observation I gave the children some magnifiers to look more closely at the balloon. These were not magnifying glasses but plastic rectangular lenses, and created additional enthusiasm. One child put a magnifier to his eyes and, rocking backwards and forwards, cried 'Oooo! Ooooo! Ooooo!' The world through a magnifier was new and novel and far more exciting than the ice balloon. The other children looked at the balloon carefully and while they did not notice the details that older children will notice (see Chapter 2) they focused on the water now puddling on the table.

It's melting.
Going away.
Getting smaller.

The exploration to this point had lasted a long time and used few resources. Some children visited the table and explored throughout that time, with no thought of other activities. Later, we put one ice balloon in a tank of water and the children were amazed that it floated. They spent some time bobbing it up and down and feeling the balloon pushing against their hands. They noticed that the balloon was getting smaller in the water and this led to further discussion about what was happening to the balloon. They decided it was 'getting smaller' because 'it's in the water'. Strangely, the children who had already acknowledged that the balloon was melting into water and that that was why there was a puddle on the table, now thought differently when the balloon was in water. When asked where the ice balloon was going they said 'into the glass', referring to the plastic of the tank. They were adamant that the ice balloon on the table was melting into water but the ice balloon in the water was melting into glass. I introduced a coloured ice balloon after this idea had

Nursery children exploring ice balloons

been expressed, but this did not influence their idea. The colour was going into the water but the ice was going into the glass. This contrasted with reception and Year 1 children (see Chapter 2) who looked strangely at me when I asked where the ice was going and answered, as if I was daft, 'In the water, of course'.

The development of children's ideas from nursery to reception and Year 1 is interesting and apparently rapid. On entering school children are likely to be more systematic in their explorations, and their ideas seem less random. In explorations of ice balloons with reception and Year 1 children, described in Chapter 2, the ideas expressed were more mature and illustrated that even a few months made considerable difference in the conceptual development of young children. They predicted that an ice balloon would melt faster in water than in the air, and that if dropped on to concrete it would smash. They were aware that when melting the ice would turn into water and that this was why the water level in the tank rose.

The final point to note with ice balloon explorations, or any

Nursery children exploring ice balloons

other explorations with children of pre-school age, is that it is important not to use too much equipment. Children should have the opportunity, and indeed are happy, to explore using their senses, and equipment to enhance their observations or aid their explorations should be used carefully. With ice balloon exploration the ice balloon alone is often enough. Magnifiers can add another dimension but are not always particularly helpful in aiding their observations. I used a tank of water with the nursery children, but another occasion could equally have seen the ice balloon being added to the water trough for normal water play.

Other explorations stem from collections of resources brought into the classroom. These can be provided by the teacher, or added to by the children. I love collections as a stimulus for exploratory work (see Chapter 2) and find that children can add new avenues

of exploration each time they are provided. A collection of electrical items used in a nursery with three- and four-year-old children created enthusiasm and opportunities to explore existing
ideas. The resources included wires with simple socket and plug
connections, 1.5 volt bulbs, 1.5 volt batteries, some switches,
buzzers and a motor. All the children knew what was needed to
make a bulb light up:

> Electric.
> Put wires in it.
> You need batteries.
> You have to plug it in here.

The difference between this exploration and the ice balloon
exploration was that the children wanted to be told 'how to do
it' and lighting the bulb became rather competitive. After some
exploring Richard managed to make a circuit and exclaimed 'I'm
the winner'. As other children lit their bulbs there were cries of
'Mine's brighter' and 'Mine's better'. There was also little interest
in sharing resources with other children. While this provided
opportunities to develop skills in working with others, care
needed to be taken to ensure that every child had a fair chance
to explore. When the circuit did not work the children tended to
say 'The battery is wrong' or 'It's broken'. These young children
had already learned to shift any possible blame from themselves.
If something did not work it was not failure on their part but
failure of resources. What a pity that we teach children that failure is a bad thing. We cannot always succeed, and failure is a
normal part of everyday life and an important stepping-stone to
success.

Lucy found that she could make her light go on and off and
this led to exploration of switches. 'That's a switch' said Richard
and Zoë picked up a switch and said, 'Like this'. Zoë then put a
switch into her circuit. 'Ooo look!' she said when it worked, and
then spent a long time turning the bulb on and off. The children
were not curious at this stage about the buzzer and motor and
did not explore these at all, being satisfied with the bulbs. Richard
eventually asked what they were for. I suggested that he put one
in his circuit and see. He put the buzzer in with the bulb and found
that they did not work. 'I need more electric' he said, and added
another battery. With a bit of assistance he made a circuit and
was delighted with his buzzer. The noise became very wearying

Nursery children exploring electricity: 'Mine lights up under the table.'

after a while, but he was developing some good ideas about circuits. Luke used the motor and added a foil propeller to make a fan. He spent the next half hour fanning people in the nursery to 'keep them cool' even though this was late October.

Collections could include artefacts from all areas of science, but may seem to be non-scientific in the same way that ice balloons are not obviously scientific. Leaves, wood samples, twigs and plants could develop ideas about the variety of living organisms, as could visits by the children's pets. A collection of bones could lead to similar development (as described later in this chapter). A collection of toys in a toy shop could lead to explorations of different toys, what they do and how they work. A collection of collage material could be explored before being used in art work. The ideas are endless and the development great.

Development of the child

We have an increasing wealth of knowledge from research to assist us in understanding the development of children. Our resulting ideas about child development are usually a mixture of our understanding of this research and our own experiences with children. My biggest influence has been the work of Piaget (1950), but my understanding has been enhanced by the work of Vygotsky (1962) and Ausubel (1968). Some of the ideas about children's conceptual development have been made accessible to teachers through the work of Donaldson (1978), and have been further developed through the work of the Children's Learning in Science (CLIS) 1982–9 and SPACE (Centre for Research in Primary Science and Technology CRIPSAT) 1986–90 projects. Although well documented, the identification of the early stages of child development merits deeper consideration with respect to the development of scientific concepts. I will do this with a constructivist Piagetian view in mind.

The sensori-motor stage of the child's development, as identified by Piaget, occurs from birth to approximately 18 months. Young children are very egocentric at this time, and are at first relatively unaware of the world around them. They appear to be limited by their simple reflex responses. They can suck and swallow, their heads move towards the warmth of the human body, their arms and legs move around in an uncontrolled manner. Soon, however, they are able to focus their eyes and recognize patterns. They recognize the human face, and this becomes a dominant part of their world. Piaget believes that at this stage children are unable to distinguish between themselves and the rest of the world. This is evidenced by their inability to recognize the existence of an object once it has been removed or hidden. As their awareness develops they are increasingly able to recognize that objects not in sight do exist and can follow an object even when it is not always visible. In this way a young child dropping a toy out of a pram will be aware of the existence and the movement of the toy even when it has fallen away from sight. The child may not remember the fallen toy for long or be aware of the possible consequences of dropping it, but when the toy has fallen the child will often look down for it.

As their awareness develops, children also become more coordinated and their movements less erratic. They learn to pick up objects and experience differences in shape, size and texture. By trial and error they are able to solve simple problems. Early toys encourage them to press buttons, fit objects into slots and generally explore a variety of phenomena. In doing this, children are developing ideas about the world around them. They are also developing useful skills for future scientific development. They are learning to look, to feel, to predict. They are also developing useful attitudes such as curiosity and perseverance. They will often sit for considerable periods of time trying to perform a task such as putting shapes into shaped slots. Once they have achieved this they will repeat it again and again. They are obviously motivated by the need to succeed. This behaviour is not seen in older children to the same extent. It may be that older children need more motivation or that they may see other activities as more appealing. They may not need to perform a task repeatedly to achieve success, although I am not convinced about this argument. It may be that many older children are not encouraged to persevere if they are unsure of success. At this early stage of development children will not have such a well-defined idea of success and will not have experienced the negative side of failure. One interpretation of the repetitive perseverance seen in young children but less in older children could be that we are developing children who can only value success and not failure. I hope not.

As children progress from the sensori-motor stage of development they move into the concrete operational stage, which will last throughout their primary school life. The concrete operational stage can be divided into two sub-stages, the pre-operational stage and the formal operational stage. The pre-operational stage will last from approximately 18 months until seven years of age, and it is at this stage that most of the early science development will occur. During this stage of development children are preparing for operations or actions in the mind. These actions are often similar at first to the physical actions carried out in the sensori-motor stage, but now children can carry them out in their minds rather than by physical means. Children begin to group, separate, order and combine in their minds in order to make sense of the world around them. These 'mind actions' can then be carried out in the physical world. At this stage children are beginning to plan for future actions, and this will have obvious use in their scientific development. For example, children will be able to predict that some objects will float in water and others will sink, but with some objects they will still need concrete experiences or to find out by trial and error. Their scientific ideas are subject to change and need reinforcement.

It is important to remember that these stages of development do not occur regardless of experiences and interaction. They are not stages in children's maturation. Like other physical stages, they will occur only if experiential opportunities are made available to children, and informed adults interact with them in an appropriate manner. In this way, a wide range of experiential opportunities should be made available from an early age to encourage development.

Children aged three and four will have had a variety of experiences which will influence their developing concepts, knowledge, skills and attitudes in science. These experiences will differ in type and context, as will their abilities to make sense of their experiences and the type and quality of the interactions within the experiences. As a result, each child is an individual with individual ideas and needs. We could say that all children have their own unique intellectual fingerprint. Each child is unique, and so we need to know as much about individual children as possible. We need to identify their skills, their attitudes and their scientific ideas. We also need to know about the experiences which have helped their development. This does not mean that we need to teach each child individually, but rather that we should recognize that each child is an individual with specific needs and abilities. Children can be grouped according to their needs and abilities, either to support and encourage development or because they have similar needs. In working with young children we need to recognize that they are not devoid of any scientific, conceptual understanding, skills or feelings about science. We need also to analyse children's ideas and behaviour and tentatively make decisions about the types of experience which will benefit them.

The acquisition of early scientific ideas

While working with three- and four-year-old children in a school nursery I was able to analyse their ideas and assign them loosely to three broad categories:

- factual knowledge;
- fictional knowledge or myths;
- inferred knowledge.

Factual knowledge can be acquired through first-hand experience or through secondary sources such as television, films or books. Children can develop factual ideas about animals from very early picture books. *The Very Hungry Caterpillar* (Carle, 1970) can develop factual knowledge about the life cycle of the butterfly. Children's television programmes can add to this information. Practical experience, observing caterpillars and butterflies in the garden at home and in the wider environment, can further develop these ideas. Fictional knowledge is acquired through secondary sources, mainly the media, tales and stories. Since factual information can also be obtained from these sources, it is easy to see why children are sometimes unable to differentiate fact from fiction. *The Very Hungry Caterpillar* contains some fictional ideas about the eating habits of the caterpillar. In the same way, children are unlikely to develop factual ideas about how to care for pets by watching or reading 'Postman Pat' stories (Cunliffe, 1987), although they may develop some fictional ideas about the habits of cats. Inferred knowledge results from an interaction between children's practical experiences and the existing ideas that they hold. These ideas may be inaccurate and can have a profound influence on further conceptual development.

All these ideas were illustrated by the nursery children I was working with. The children were given a collection of bones to explore. These included skulls from a sheep, a cow, a rat and a human, vertebrae from a horse and a rabbit, a cow's femur, the jaw bone from a dog, a whale's tooth and other assorted teeth in and out of skulls, horns from a sheep and a deer, and a collection of shells of various types. The children freely visited the table where I had placed this collection of bones, and they explored them with great excitement. In their initial observations they expressed their factual knowledge through their comments. In picking up the femur of a cow one child said 'Bones are for dogs', while another said 'Dogs eat bones'. While looking at the collection of shells the children said 'Crabs live in shells' and 'Shells come from the seaside'. Observation of a large cow's horn led to the following dialogue between a group of three children.

> Horns come from animals. (*Putting the horn on the side of his head.*) A cow.
> (*Putting the horn on his nose.*) Rhinoceros! Rhinoceros!
> (*Picking up a deer's horn.*) Reindeer!
> (*Holding a sheep's horn.*) Here's another one.

One child later drew a picture of the deer's horn and asked for it to be annotated with the words 'This is a deer's horn. It's got a straight bit. It goes on your head.'

While illustrating their knowledge as to the types of animals possessing horns, this dialogue also demonstrated an early classification skill, in verbally grouping the horns. This was further demonstrated by the children's recognition of teeth, in and out of animal skulls. The teeth were similar in type and shape, the exception being the whale's tooth. However, the children classified the latter as both a tooth and a horn at different times and were quite happy with its dual role. The children also grouped the shells together. Their ability to group things together illustrated the development of a rule or theory about the objects: the various shells and teeth may be different in type, texture and shape but they have features in common which make them recognizably shells or teeth. It seems that classificatory decisions are made on the basis of observations but that contextual clues may be important, as with teeth in the skulls or jaw bones.

Fictional information or myths can become mixed up with factual information. Sometimes this information is acquired through first-hand experiences combined with creativity and imagination, as with the child who informed me that 'You can hear the sea in shells.' Sometimes this information comes from stories in books and through the media. While exploring the collections of bones, shells and teeth one child, influenced by ghostly stories or picture books such as *Funnybones* (Ahlberg and Ahlberg, 1980), said 'Skeletons come in the night.' Sometimes factual and fictional sources combine to provide accurate knowledge such as the child influenced by the 'Spot' books who drew a picture of the cow's femur and asked me to annotate with the words 'Spot's bone. You get bones from the country; I've seen one.'

In the bone exploration the children illustrated inferred knowledge through the following comments, together with their actions.

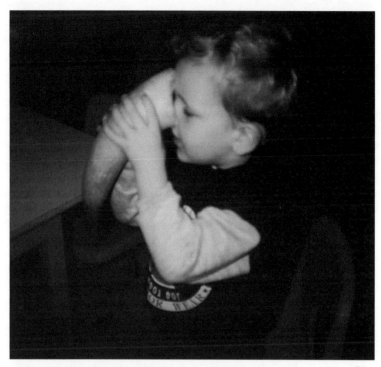

Nursery children exploring bones: 'Rhinoceros! Rhinoceros!'

(*Looking at the jaw of the dog.*) This must be its chin.
(*Looking at the teeth in the dog's jaw.*) It's from a shark.
(*Looking at the eye sockets in a skull.*) These must be eyes.

One child, without making any comment, put the horns at the side of the skulls and then his own head, while another child commented 'They go here.'

The conceptual and linguistic development of these children had been fairly rapid. Within four years they had learnt from a variety of experiences about the world around them. They had learnt through experience and, most importantly, the learning had meaning for them. It was relevant to their lives. Donaldson (1978: 121) recognizes the importance of relevance when she says that 'children can show skill as thinkers and language-users to a degree which must compel our respect, so long as they are dealing with "real-life" meaningful situations'.

In providing experiences for children we need to consider how relevant they are to their lives and make the purpose of the learning explicit where possible. Recently an adult recalled his nursery experiences to me, describing them as 'boring, boring, boring'. He felt that young science experiences were not worthwhile because they were quickly forgotten, but he went on to tell me about his one positive and memorable experience from nursery. Each day he was asked to turn the sand in the sand pit to allow the sun to dry it out. He was told that this was a very important job because otherwise the children would only be able to play in wet, cold sand. He could see the relevance of the job and its importance grew as a result. It was a pity he did not see the science in the activity, but the anecdote really emphasized for me the importance of relevant science exploration. Some children do not need this amount of relevance. They can learn and enjoy experiences for aesthetic reasons, but we need to provide both relevant and aesthetic experiences for young learners to help to develop their full potential.

Children develop their ideas through a variety of experiences throughout their early lives. Piaget's ideas have been extremely influential in developing our understanding of children's learning. Piaget and other psychologists and educational thinkers have informed us about the needs of children in the development of their concepts and this knowledge has enabled us, for the most part, to make informed educational and pre-educational decisions which aid learning. Vygotsky placed emphasis on the importance of language development in the formation of concepts. Ausubel's theory of meaningful learning has formed the basis for much recent research into how children learn and the importance of their early ideas as a basis for future conceptual development. Fleer (1993) has identified the rise in interest in young children's scientific learning but she also identifies a lack of research into the development of scientific ideas in the very young. Indeed, most research appears to focus on children above the age of eight. Despite this the research has been useful in identifying misconceptions and development trends. Along with many other teachers I have found the constructivist approach to be most useful in my teaching. While the constructivist approach to learning in science seems to take many forms and the word does appear to mean different things to different people, Scott (1987) describes my view of constructivism. He stresses the importance of the teacher knowing children's existing ideas and the children's role in developing their own ideas, constructing their own meanings. Learning at any age is not a passive act. There needs to be a willingness to learn, a motivating force and then some kind of commitment to learn. Early explorations are the key to future scientific development, providing interest, motivation and practical experience. These ideas will be developed in more detail in later chapters of this book. Chapter 2 looks at the nature of exploration in some detail. Chapter 3 looks at the importance and the problems of motivation through creative activities. Chapter 4 looks at the development of attitudes in and to science and the part played by explorations. Finally, Chapter 5 focuses on the role of the teacher in the exploratory process.

Summary

- Pre-school scientific concepts, skills and attitudes develop rapidly. There are many factors which influence scientific development in young children.
- Pre-school ideas appear to develop as a result of a combination of factual, fictional and inferred knowledge, acquired in a variety of ways.
- The importance of pre-school scientific knowledge should not be underestimated, as it may have a profound effect on future scientific development.

Useful reading

Isaacs, N. (1961) *The Growth of Understanding in the Young Child: A Brief Introduction to Piaget's Work*. London: Ward Lock Educational.

2

---

*The importance of
exploration in the development
of early years science
knowledge and skills*

I am a firm believer in exploration as an important element in
teaching and learning. I believe that exploration plays a vital part
in the development of both early years scientific skills and knowledge and is a prerequisite for more in-depth development of
skills and knowledge, especially in children of primary school age.

What do we mean by the word *exploration*? Dictionaries describe it by using such words as *hunt, research, investigation, pursuit,
enquiry, chase* and *quest*. Other words such as *discovery, inspira-
tion* and *revelation* stress its creative aspects (Figure 2.1). The
process of exploration is also associated with a lack of any expecta-
tion or preconceptions and with experiential learning, which, as
I hope to demonstrate, is the most effective way to establish
understanding.

The importance of the scientific process was recognized before
the implementation of the National Curriculum, with an emphasis
on the development of skills by primary science projects and pub-

Figure 2.1 What is exploration?

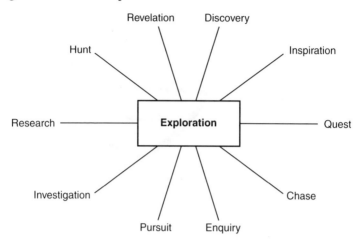

lications such as the Nuffield Foundation Junior Science Project (1964–6), the Schools Council Science 5/13 Project (1967–74), Harlen (1977a; 1977b), Symington (1978) and Jelly (1985). The National Curriculum (see Table 1.1) has endorsed this emphasis on the scientific process and the development of skills since its inception. In 1989, the Department of Education and Science (DES) recommended that Attainment Target 1, Exploration of Science, had a weighting of 50% at Key Stage 1. This was further endorsed in Circular 17/91 (DES, 1991a) when the amended Science Orders recommended a 50% weighting for the new Attainment Target 1, Scientific Investigation. In the classroom, this has meant that the development of concepts and knowledge in science at Key Stages 1 and 2 should occur as a result of practical experiences. The relationship between exploration and investigation, on the one hand, and scientific concepts and knowledge, on the other, can be likened to a double helix, both developing in linked spirals (Figure 2.2). This reminds me of Confucius' saying, 'I hear and I forget, I see and I remember, I do and I understand.' Surely the point of our work is to develop in children positive scientific attitudes, along with an understanding of scientific concepts, the skills of science and the nature of science, so that any attempt to reduce the weighting for exploration and investigation at Key Stages 1 and 2 must be deplored. I also deeply regret the name changes, from Exploration of Science through Scientific

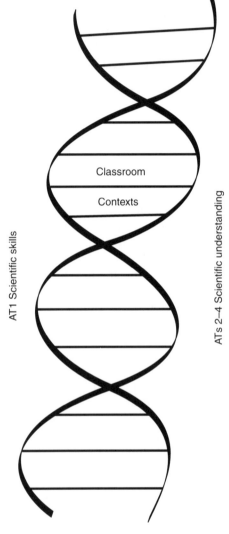

Figure 2.2 The development of scientific understanding and scientific skills

AT1 Scientific skills

ATs 2–4 Scientific understanding

Classroom

Contexts

Investigation to Experimental and Investigative Science, as this appears to neglect the importance of exploration in science. The words 'exploration', 'investigation' and 'experimentation' have very different meanings. The change of name to 'Experimental and Investigative Science' was an intentional attempt to emphasize both experimentation and investigation which are important for secondary science education. As a result 'exploration' is now felt to be unimportant and primary teachers feel it is not a necessary part of the primary science process. Exploration is a common strand in the different learning models in science. Cosgrove and Osborne (1985) provide a useful summary of learning models in science, a number of which involve exploration, albeit under different guises; Renner's (1982) 'experiences' provided by the teacher, Karplus's (1977) 'exploration' with minimal guidance and Erikson's (1979) 'experimental manoeuvres' are all examples of exploration in science. Cosgrove and Osborne also describe their own model, 'generative learning', which emphasizes exploration as a 'precondition to successful science learning' (Cosgrove and Osborne, 1985: 106), encouraging curiosity and motivating the desire for further enquiry.

Early explorations are often apparently unsystematic and seemingly unproductive, reflecting children's lack of maturity at this stage, but as children mature, there is a development of exploratory skills which enables more skilled exploration and planned investigation to occur. In this way exploration plays a very important part in the scientific process by helping to develop exploratory skills such as observation, classification, raising questions and hypothesizing. These skills are important first steps in the development of other skills in the scientific process, especially planning, predicting and investigating (Figure 2.3). They are additionally important in the development of positive attitudes to science, discussed in Chapter 4.

Observation

Observation is a skill which, I believe, we are very poor in developing effectively, despite the fact that we acknowledge it as an important part of science. This is not meant as a criticism of teaching strategies and does need further consideration and explanation, especially given the apparent contradictions in Harlen

Figure 2.3   The scientific process

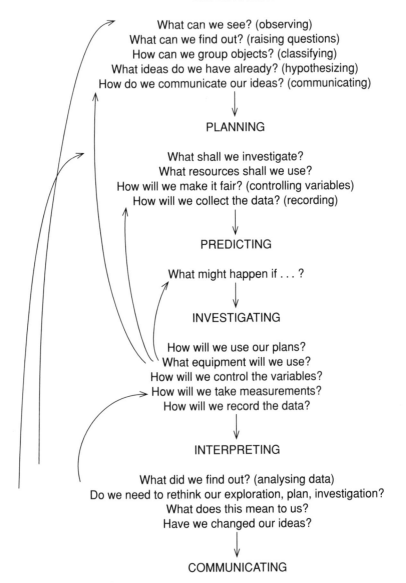

EXPLORATION

What can we see? (observing)
What can we find out? (raising questions)
How can we group objects? (classifying)
What ideas do we have already? (hypothesizing)
How do we communicate our ideas? (communicating)

PLANNING

What shall we investigate?
What resources shall we use?
How will we make it fair? (controlling variables)
How will we collect the data? (recording)

PREDICTING

What might happen if . . . ?

INVESTIGATING

How will we use our plans?
What equipment will we use?
How will we control the variables?
How will we take measurements?
How will we record the data?

INTERPRETING

What did we find out? (analysing data)
Do we need to rethink our exploration, plan, investigation?
What does this mean to us?
Have we changed our ideas?

COMMUNICATING

Can we explain what we did, found out, changed?

and Symington (1985). One view is that observation is something that children are very good at but that, as they develop, they begin to simplify the world, 'filtering out' things they believe to be unimportant because the world becomes too large for them to observe everything. This filtering out of observations can be seen in many aspects of concept development and is an important part of the scientific process, whereby the scientist focuses on those observations of particular relevance to the investigation. As this ability to filter out observations progresses, adults and developing children do not always recognize what they observe. What is important is that we are able to make broad observations before we begin to focus on specific observations. Harlen and Symington seem to agree with both this and my opening sentence in this section when they qualify their statement that observation is highly rated in education and is recognized as important in science activities by arguing that 'there is a case for helping children to observe more effectively and to focus on the teacher's role in improving observational skills' (Harlen and Symington, 1985: 21). My claim that observation is a skill which we are very poor in developing effectively originated as a result of personal observations of the deterioration in children's observational skills and reflects these viewpoints. Children appear to move from unsophisticated general observations to unsophisticated particular observations, rather than improve their skills in both types of observation.

I feel we can also look at the demands on teaching more specifically when analysing why observational skills do not improve as desired. One reason may be that the demands of modern teaching tend to focus on the organization of science activities and the development of knowledge. We seem to be on a treadmill of teaching and learning; we keep running in order to ensure content coverage, while understanding, resulting from quality exploration and investigation, gets left behind. We need to focus on the reality that quality learning is more important than the amount of content covered. Young children are very good observers, especially while interacting (Goldsworthy, 1989). As part of explorations, they will, characteristically, make use of their senses, notice details, identify similarities and differences between objects and events, put events in the correct sequence and begin to use observational aids (Harlen, 1992). Poor observation has been linked to a lack of curiosity or to over-activity (Harlen, 1977a; 1977b), so that children who, for whatever reason, are withdrawn or over-active do not allow themselves the same opportunities to observe. Nursery and Key Stage 1 children are often very perceptive observers. In observations of ice balloons children have likened the radiating bubbles of air inside the balloons to 'the inside of a peach' and 'hair'. These observations can only be based on the children's previous experiences and, as a result, are obviously limited, but they are also very creative and imaginative observations. This creative aspect of children's observations should be encouraged. It is important that we do not impose our own beliefs, which arise from our limited experiences, on children's observations and that we help them to develop confidence in their observations.

Observational skills and creativity can also be seen through children's drawings. For example, when drawing pictures of fish from observation, Rebecca noted the patterns of their scales and made up her own pattern. When drawing a plant, Sarah put it into a decorative pot in her bedroom. In both situations, the detailed observation was not lessened by the creative additions but in fact indicated wider powers of observation.

I believe that older children are less able to be creative in their observations and that this is, in part, to do with our teaching. As children develop they learn a great deal about the world around them from hidden messages, from body language and through interpretation. They appear to receive messages about observation in science which devalue creativity and imagination: 'Is your hair really green?', 'Why have you drawn it like this?' The result is that they observe those things they feel we value and they do not often include creative and imaginative ideas or observations. The message about the nature of science, as being cold, unimaginative and uncreative, seems to contradict children's drawings of scientists which often include evidence of imaginative thought and new creative ideas through the inclusion of Eureka bubbles and light bulbs (Figure 2.4; see also Chambers, 1983).

Raising questions

Opportunities for explorations and observations can lead to children raising questions. Research by Symington (1978: 172) showed that exploration can lead to 'a very significant increase in

Figure 2.4 A child's picture of a scientist

the number of investigable scientific problems' being put forward by children. Raising questions is a skill which comes naturally to most young children, and in a learning context the types of question we are attempting to elicit are ones which will promote new explorations and allow investigation. As such, raising questions is central to exploration. It is also a skill closely involved with making judgements about children and assessing their ideas. This is because the questions children raise are likely to indicate gaps in their experience or misconceptions they hold.

However, raising questions is not a skill which appears to develop with age. A visitor to a nursery or a Key Stage 1 classroom will be met by a barrage of questions – who? what? how? and, especially, why? In a Year 6 class, despite the development of higher-order skills, questions do not trip readily off the children's tongues. In many ways, the reason for this anomaly lies in the nature of both society and the primary classroom.

As children develop, there can be more sources of information available to them and they do not always need to ask questions to obtain an answer. There are also influences on them which deter them from asking questions. A very important influence is self image, which is greatly influenced by peer pressure. Asking questions can portray an image which is unacceptable to a child's peers: the child either doesn't know the answer and so is stupid, or wants to know the answer and so is a swot. In a competitive society it is better not to compete than to fail, and in raising questions you definitely cannot win. Children also learn that their questions are often not answered, so that asking questions becomes a pointless exercise. Additionally, asking questions can lead to further work, with teachers using a child's question to stimulate discussion and focus on further exploration or investigation. The only acceptable question for older children is one which distracts the teacher and avoids work. For the teacher, children raising questions can also be a cause for concern, especially in science explorations. The familiar cry of 'What if I don't know the answer myself?' is heard throughout primary classrooms, and it is very hard to persuade teachers that it is both unrealistic and unnecessary to expect them to know all the answers.

In some ways I sympathize with teachers in this situation – we all want to feel secure in our teaching and to provide the best for the children in our classes. Knowledge gives us that security. It is no longer possible to imagine that one person could possess all the knowledge about the multitude of disciplines we call science. Furthermore, it would provide a false picture to children in the classroom if they were led to believe that it was possible for one person to know everything and that their teacher was that person. This, however, is of little practical help in the classroom when faced with a question you cannot answer. In such a situation there are some strategies which I have found useful.

The first is honesty, to admit that you don't really know, or haven't thought about the problem in a particular way. The next strategy is to ask the child for his or her ideas and to begin to explore the issue together. You may not come up with a definite answer but, in doing this, you clearly emphasize a view of the nature of science which is often incompatible with children's views. We need to move away from the view that science is a precise methodology and a body of laws or facts which, if known, logically explain everything.

Challenging the children's ideas will help to develop a more realistic view of the nature of science. I choose to encourage the view that science is concerned with developing ideas about the world; the best ideas are the ones you hold until they are challenged by experiences, after which you change, modify or develop them. The child who decided that the ice balloon stuck to the table because a piece of balloon was underneath it (see Chapter 1) developed ideas as a result of experience and needed further experience to challenge these ideas.

The final strategy is to research the question, either with the child or independently, and return to it later. I was once asked a difficult question about planetary motion by a teacher on an in-service course and, not wishing to give a false answer, I admitted my ignorance and immediately rang the Education Officer at Jodrell Bank, who very kindly gave us an immediate answer. Obviously, this strategy will be less successful if tried with a class of five-year-old children, who will not wait while you find out and whose interest in the answer will be lost quickly anyway. However, further personal research does take you further up the learning curve, and you will be able to answer that question next time! There are a number of informed bodies and associations which can help you in answering those tricky questions. Education officers at science centres, science institutes and professional associations such as the Association for Science Education can all be of help.

The key to developing the skill of raising questions is to provide an atmosphere in your classroom where children feel able to practise that skill. In such an atmosphere you can then encourage children to examine their questions in order to see if they can be answered by further exploration, investigation or research, which of course develops other skills in the scientific process.

Classification

Classification skills can be developed through observation and exploration; such skills are, indeed, necessary before children can effectively investigate further. In order to be able to carry out an investigation successfully children need to be able to see similarities and differences between objects and events and to rearrange them according to features they have in common; in other words, to classify them. Classifying things reduces the number of different impressions children have and allows them to learn from experiences, enabling them to make sense of the world around them. Recognizing the stages in the development of children's classificatory ideas allows us to assist with their learning. At an early stage of their development, children will put objects into groups, but will be unable to give reasons for the groupings which make sense of their actions. These objects 'go together' rather than have a shared feature. They may recognize a feature which distinguishes them but may be unable to communicate this. A further development is when children use one feature as a basis for grouping. For example, when exploring a collection of toy vehicles a young child may focus on the red vehicles and will then group all the red vehicles together in one group and then all the other vehicles in another group, regardless of colour. At the next developmental stage children will decide upon a single criterion, such as colour, which differentiates all the vehicles. They will then be able to make several groups, for example, red cars, blue cars, green cars. As children notice that objects can have more than one property at the same time, they become able to classify them and then to reclassify them because of another criterion. Taking cars as an example, criteria could include colour, shape, make, usage, speed and number of passengers. In order to classify objects according to two criteria simultaneously, children need to be able to keep two ideas in mind at the same time. The exploration of a collection of vehicles could lead to investigating the distance travelled by different vehicles down a ramp which is covered with different surfaces.

Children who have developed well the skill of classification should be able to identify objects or conditions with a combination of features, without going through the whole classification process. This ability is basic to logical thinking, particularly to undertaking investigations in science which involve separating variables. Young children should be provided with opportunities for exploration which enable them to handle simple variables. The most simple explorations involve categoric variables. These allow us clearly to identify variables, usually according to observable features such as colour or shape. For example, in our investigation to see which toy vehicle travels the furthest down a ramp the categorical variables are the shape and colour of the cars. This can lead to consideration of fair testing, where children need to identify the key variables; that is, they must identify what they are changing (the independent variable), in this case the vehicle, and what happens as a result or is affected by the change (the dependent variable), in this case the distance travelled.

These are the variables which define an investigation and their complexity can affect the difficulty of the investigation. A categoric variable, such as the colour or type of car, is the simplest, but variables can be much more complex. If we are interested in the distance travelled by each vehicle (the dependent variable), then we are introducing the difficulty of needing to measure the distance, although the use of non-standard measures in early explorations can alleviate this difficulty. Changing the dependent variable to investigate the speed of each vehicle makes the investigation more complex still, because speed has to be calculated from two measurements, distance and time, and is therefore a derived variable. Simple investigations have a smaller number of additional variables to control. These additional variables, or control variables, need to remain constant throughout in order to make the investigation fair. In our vehicle investigation these would include the height of the ramp, the way the vehicle is released, and the surface over which it travels.

Other investigations may involve not just more complex variables but more than one independent and dependent variable. For example, in an investigation to see how far vehicles of different weights travel down a ramp, the independent variable is the type of vehicle and the dependent variable is the distance travelled. If, however, the investigation is changed slightly and the weight of each vehicle and the height of the ramp are considered to see how they make a difference to the distance travelled, then there are two independent variables, vehicle weight and ramp height. Thus the investigation becomes more complex. In another variation, the vehicle weight may be the independent variable but there may be two dependent variables such as distance and time, and these can be calculated to discover the speed of each vehicle, making a third derived dependent variable.

In a typical investigation at this level, Year 1 and 2 children decided to find out whose hands were the largest. They decided to use a tub of marbles and see how many marbles they could pick up. Each child used one hand to pick up the marbles and the number of marbles picked up was counted and recorded. In this investigation the independent variable was the hand used to pick up the marbles. The dependent variable was the number of marbles picked up. In order to make this investigation fair a number of other variables needed to be controlled. These control variables included the tub of marbles, which needed to remain constant for each child, and the way the children picked up the marbles, whether they scooped them up (with the palm of the hand up) or grabbed them (with the palm of the hand down). In this investigation the variables concerned were simple and there was one independent and one dependent variable.

Obviously for young children we do not want complex invest-igation with a large number of variables to control. Young chil-dren will need to begin with simple investigations with few and simple variables, and the complexity should increase with their ability to recognize and handle variables. This does not mean that a vehicle investigation is too complex for young children, but rather that we need to plan carefully for the investigation and ensure that children are not frustrated by the complexity of the variables. Goldsworthy and Feasey (1994) identify the pro-gression in handling variables and making investigations fair. From open explorations children observe differences and raise questions. This leads to simple investigations where the teacher controls the variables but allows opportunities to consider whether the test is fair or unfair. 'It was fair because we all did it the same way', is a familiar statement from young children. Further devel-opment allows children to handle some variables in an invest-igation, but other variables need controlling for the children. Our desired goal is for children to plan and carry out investigations having identified and controlled all the variables whatever their complexity.

Hypothesizing

Through explorations and simple investigations, children begin to develop simple hypotheses. A hypothesis is an explanation for a scientific event or feature; it differs from a prediction, which states what will happen next or in the future. In explorations of vehicles, all children predicted that the vehicles would go down the ramp but they all had different hypotheses as to why. Carl, aged seven, developed the simple hypothesis that the shape of the vehicle made it go fast: 'The car goes down the ramp because it's triangle shaped.' Katherine, aged five, considered friction when she said the vehicle went down the ramp 'because it slides'; and Gareth, aged six, had some early ideas about gravity when he said that the vehicle went down the ramp 'because the ramp's like a big hill and it's falling down'.

Exploration in the water trough can lead to simple hypotheses about floating and sinking. For many children these hypotheses concern the weight of the object, such as 'It will sink because it's heavy' and 'If you put something really heavy on it, it'll sink.'

These ideas develop as a result of previous experiences in school and out. The swimming pool, boat trips and bath time all play an important part in developing these hypotheses. Tracey, who had been on a ship, had developed a hypothesis that heavy things floated because of the depth of the water. Jon had noticed that a swimming float 'pushed' against his hand and he thought it might be the 'water pushing'. Floating and sinking was the focus of the first reported year of Standard Assessment Tasks for seven-year-old children in 1990. My son, Andrew, was involved in these, and as they were very practical assessments they provided ample opportunity for children to express their ideas gained through previous explorations and investigations. Andrew came home from school extremely excited about the floating and sinking activities. He had been asked to predict which objects, from a range supplied, would float or sink.

> I had to say what things would float and what would sink. . . .
> I thought that all the heavy things would sink and all the
> light things would float. I had a shell that weighed 5 grams
> and a cork that weighed 55 grams and I thought the shell
> would float and the cork would sink.

He had not only predicted which object would float or sink, he had offered his hypothesis about floating and sinking: heavy things sink and light things float. He continued: 'But I was wrong! The cork floated and the shell sank, but I think I know why.' He didn't need much encouragement to give me his new hypothesis and his reasoning:

> Well, I know an ice balloon is very heavy. [He had made
> one at home with me.] I could hardly lift it up and it floated
> in the bucket and I know that a ship is very very heavy and
> I couldn't pick it up. Well . . . I think that when something
> is light it floats and when it is heavy it sinks but when it gets
> very heavy it floats again.

Andrew's hypotheses, although not matching the scientific theories, were developed through exploration and investigation. Further practical experience would be needed to try out his new hypothesis about floating and sinking and to provide challenges for it. It is important to remember that a hypothesis does not have to be correct but should 'be reasonable in terms of the evidence available and possible in terms of scientific concepts or principles' (Harlen, 1992: 30). For Andrew, further exploration and investigation was needed to try out his hypothesis and attempt to modify his ideas.

Communication

Exploration can provide a forum for children to develop their ideas about science as well as in science and can provide opportunities to communicate these ideas. Communication is a very important skill to develop in young children (Barnes, 1976). In science, Harlen (1985: 39) describes communication as 'an outward extension of thought'. It is essential that children are given time to think about their explorations and are given opportunities to express their ideas. This enables them to sort out any muddled thinking: to clarify their ideas and reach a better understanding. Children need to clarify their ideas in order to communicate them to others, and communication often encourages them to evaluate their ideas. Often, we undertake scientific activities with children but forget to think carefully about the ideas being developed. The pressures of the busy classroom seem to dictate that we move on quickly to the next set of ideas and the children's ideas remain half-formed or muddled. Communicating these ideas will help children to be clearer about them. Communication also gives children access to the ideas of others. These, too, may be partially formed and they may conflict with ideas already held, but it is important that children learn to consider their own ideas as tentative and subject to change and this is often the first occasion when this can occur. They may agree with the ideas expressed, they may disagree, but it is important that they think about how they match with their own ideas. If the ideas expressed by others challenge their own beliefs they may feel confused and unhappy and need to undertake a period of further exploration and investigation. In many scientific explorations this communication consists of the general talking which is associated with any classroom activity – the classroom buzz. This is constructive talk where children bounce ideas off each other, express and clarify their ideas, and in the process reach a deeper understanding. A quiet classroom is often not the best environment for learning to occur.

The role of the teacher in facilitating this communication is of great importance. Situations need to be provided where children can discuss their ideas. This may involve the whole class or a small group of children. The advantage of small groups is that children can all be involved in a meaningful way and are less likely to feel intimidated by the more dominant members of the group. The advantage of a larger group is that there are more ideas to challenge the children and promote discussion, although situations where all children take turns in expressing their ideas can be time-consuming and demotivating for children. It is more important for children to listen to others and to contribute to the discussion than to have a turn for, as Harlen (1992: 105) says, if communication 'is mainly a social event, with the emphasis on the opportunity to speak and little feedback in relation to the content, then it may become something of a ritual'. Carpet time can provide the occasion for children to review their work and ideas and think about new explorations and investigations.

I have sometimes enabled carpet time to be developmental rather than informative by organizing explorations to develop from the ideas arising from others. Groups of children are given the opportunity to explore a collection of materials over the course of a week. Normally this type of activity would be organized so that, after a brief introduction to the whole class, at the beginning of the week, each group starts afresh and looks at the materials as if for the first time. By the time the final group of children undertake the activity, they have been aware of the resources and the other children's interactions, albeit on an informal classroom observational basis. While there is nothing wrong with this approach, an alternative method of organization can be motivating, leading to greater development of knowledge skills and attitudes, and this can be facilitated through better communication. Using the carpet time effectively, the activity to explore the collection of materials and to make observations and raise questions about them can be introduced. The first group of children can then communicate their observations and ideas about the materials in a subsequent carpet time. All the children in the class can then be encouraged to look for interesting anomalies or patterns in the ideas expressed and to analyse them. This can lead to a decision as to what questions can be answered during the next group's exploration and may lead to some investigation. Feedback from the second group's exploration can promote new ideas and discussion which in turn can help another group to begin to plan an investigation. As a result, the whole class is immersed in the work of all, and cooperation and the sharing of ideas take on new meaning.

I do not suggest that this is a method of organization that is desirable in every situation or should replace the individual development that should occur when children individually explore, raise questions, investigate, develop hypotheses and communicate their ideas to others. Also, as Goldsworthy and Feasey (1994) indicate, young children do not find analysis of their ideas easy. It therefore becomes important that situations are provided which allow them to communicate their ideas in a supportive atmosphere, not in a situation where the teacher dominates (Elstgeest *et al.*, 1985).

Scientific knowledge

An open-ended exploratory activity will provide children with opportunities to pursue avenues of enquiry which are of interest to them and allow them to formulate simple hypotheses about their experiences. In an exploratory activity, children engage in observations, raising questions from their observations which can be explored further or which may involve more systematic investigation. As a result of the exploration, children choose differentiated pathways to follow which are consistent with their needs and abilities. There will be a number of learning outcomes, but in each case the outcome is likely to be relevant to the children's learning needs. A more prescriptive activity will involve all children undertaking an identical or slightly differentiated activity, leading to one learning outcome. This learning outcome may not be consistent with every child's needs and abilities and, as a result, some children may not further develop their knowledge or skills; moreover, there may be an element of disillusion or frustration.

This can be illustrated by the following observation of a group of Year 2 children who were looking at magnetism. They had embarked on an activity which was designed to develop knowledge about which materials were magnetic and which non-magnetic. It involved the children in testing a range of objects and putting a tick or cross beside a picture on a worksheet. The children quickly engaged in, and completed, the task and were then allowed some time for exploration using the resources provided. One child quickly observed that the magnet worked through the table and very excitedly began to investigate which other materials, and which thicknesses of materials, the magnet worked through. Another child observed through her play that the magnet made a paper clip 'jump off the table' when placed above it. She then went on to observe that 'it didn't do it' when the paper clip was placed on a pair of scissors, but the paper clip could be made to 'stand up'. She hypothesized that it was 'the scissors that made it do it', although she could not explain why. A third child had obviously developed a theory that magnets attract all metal objects and, even though the original activity had challenged this by using a variety of metallic objects, he still clung on to this theory. His ideas were, however, challenged by the exploration because he was unable to ignore those objects that challenged him. He decided that all the metal objects which were not attracted to the magnet must be 'aluma', and it was clear that his experiences had included recycling aluminium drink cans. However, he also felt that 'aluma' was a metal and therefore his observations did not fit his theory. At this point, he became very confused and ready to investigate a range of metallic objects to see which types of metal were attracted to the magnet. This exploratory activity was originally perceived by the student teacher as a 'filler', and she was exceptionally surprised to notice how much quality learning was developed compared to the original planned activity.

Another observation of reception and Year 1 children, who were involved in an investigation of materials, illustrates the importance of exploration before investigation to maximize understanding. The investigation involved the children in using a variety of writing implements (pencil, ballpoint pen, felt-tip pen and wax crayon) and a variety of surfaces (plastic, blotting paper, writing paper and wallpaper) and was structured to help control variables. The children had to stick strips of the material on a prepared worksheet and write their name on them using each type of writing implement. It was a lovely, imaginative way to record an investigation, but some children were unsure of the reason for the activity, and when asked what they were doing responded with 'We are learning to write our names' or 'I don't know'. Other children found the activity difficult because they did not understand the worksheet categories or could not fit their names in the spaces provided. All children would have benefited from an initial period of exploration, allowing them to try out different writing implements and surfaces and being encouraged to develop hypotheses about the suitability of the surfaces and the implements, before investigating further and recording those investigations.

Explorations can identify for us conceptual areas in need of clarification, modification or development. To do this successfully, we need to have a clear understanding of the relevant concept ourselves and be able to identify the common ideas held by children. There is a plethora of very useful research on children's ideas that we can draw upon, especially the research resulting from the Children's Learning in Science (CLIS) project at Leeds University's Centre for Studies in Science and Mathematics Education, and the Primary Science Processes and Concept Exploration (SPACE) project at Liverpool University's Centre for Research in Primary Science and Technology (CRIPSAT) and King's College London's Centre for Educational Studies. In order to assist children effectively in their explorations and develop their scientific concepts, we need to be able to perceive the ideas from a child's perspective. This perspective will reflect the child's previous experiences and may be very limited in nature. Children have fewer experiences to bring to any situation than adults, and often things adults take for granted can be confusing and create misconceptions. As a result, in all explorations, we need to take care that we look carefully at the children's developing ideas from their perspective. For example, let us consider how explorations of materials can illustrate some of the differing ideas that children hold and how they can give an insight into their perceptions.

I often begin explorations of materials with a mixed bag of household shopping. This can lead to children's explorations involving classification according to material properties (hard, soft, squidgy, rough, smooth, liquid, solid, gas), origin (naturally occurring, man-made, processed, plant, animal, country) or use (washing, eating, making). When exploring materials, confusions can arise because some words have different meanings in a scientific context than in everyday use. For example, what does the word 'material' mean to a child? Does it mean matter, textiles, fabric? I once asked a child who had been asked to write a sentence using the word 'liquid' what she thought the word meant.

She was quite confident in her answer that it was 'something that was used for washing up or was used in washing machines'. In the same way, what does a child think a gas is? A fuel for fires and cookers? Does a child consider both a piece of wood and a ball of plasticine to be solid? They do not look the same; one is malleable and the other is not; one is hard and the other is not, but both are considered solid in the scientific sense.

Another cause of confusion may occur when exploring naturally occurring or man-made materials as this is an abstract idea which many children will not have experienced. I well remember my daughter, at about five years of age, telling me in amazement that her grandmother made chips from potatoes! In our bag of shopping we need to realize that most naturally occurring products are processed by man and look decidedly dissimilar to their natural state. For example, a can and a sheet of foil made of aluminium look dissimilar and neither looks like a lump of bauxite; cardboard does not look like a tree; cheese does not look like milk; and plastic does not look like oil. If the aim in our explorations is to consider whether the material is naturally occurring, man-made or processed, we need to have a range of artefacts for comparison which include material in its natural state and, where possible, materials within the children's experience – for example, sheep's wool, rocks, tree branches or twigs – otherwise we need to change our criteria for classification to include naturally occurring materials which have been processed by man. This obviously changes the nature of exploration with a bag of shopping, but we need to be prepared for the possible ideas emerging from such an exploration.

From such a starting point, other materials in their natural state or processed in a different way can be introduced. Follow-up work with a bag of shopping often involves simple baking investigations to see if the materials change during the baking process and to consider whether these changes are reversible or not. Materials in the bag of shopping which are considered to exhibit a reversible change of state when heated or cooled (for example, chocolate and butter) can be compared with others which are considered to be irreversible (for example, eggs and fruit). To a child some of these reversible changes are confusing. A bar of chocolate or a pat of butter melted and allowed to cool does not look the same after these changes even if in scientific terms it is a reversible change.

Curiosity

The importance of positive attitudes to science is discussed further in Chapter 4; here we can say that exploration can also help in their development. Allowing children opportunities to explore encourages them to be curious, open-minded, creative and inventive. Perhaps the most important attitude for exploration is curiosity. Curious children have the need to know about everything they interact with, and this leads to the ability to raise questions and to investigate. Not all children display curiosity, and this needs to be encouraged in school if children are to benefit fully from their explorations. Harlen (1977b) has identified four possible causes for a lack of curiosity in children: temperament, experience, environment and social constraints. These factors interact to make the identification of causes difficult. Quiet children in an unfamiliar context, newly arrived in school and with low self-confidence, may appear to be lacking in curiosity but it may be that their reserve hides their interest. Similarly, children whose previous experiences have discouraged them from exploring or who have previously had their over-zealous curiosity suppressed may not choose to be curious or, at least, overtly curious. While very young children can spend long periods of time exploring (see Chapter 1), as the world opens up to them children will be attracted to new situations. In the midst of so many new experiences their curiosity is often short-lived and they quickly move on to the next situation. As they develop, their interest will be sustained for longer periods of time and they make use of all their senses, and it is often at this stage that a multitude of questions are raised which are seemingly impossible to answer or investigate. Further development leads to detailed observations and the need to understand.

When introducing new experiences into a Key Stage 1 classroom I have been met with exclamations of 'Ooo, what is it?', 'Is it a . . . ?', 'Do they . . . ?', 'Can we . . . ?' and even 'What do we do with it?' and 'What does it do?' In addition, a mass of hands are wanting to delve in and explore. This is not, however, the situation for all children in the class. There are always some who appear not to show an interest or choose not to explore or who, during carpet-time discussions, sit quietly waiting for the end. Children should be encouraged to display curiosity, by being encouraged to observe closely, explore and raise questions. For this to occur satisfactorily, time needs to be set aside for quality exploration of a range of different phenomena. These can be from within the children's experience, where they are able to look at the familiar in a different way, or new phenomena, the exploration of which may need encouragement for less confident children. Once children are curious enough to explore and are able to listen to the ideas of others, knowing they are valued, they will become more open-minded and tolerant and will feel more confident about expressing their ideas.

Examples of exploratory activities

Having identified how important exploration is, as a prerequisite to investigation it would be useful to look at some examples of good explorations – explorations which can lead to good investigations. Explorations with ice balloons are a favourite because the context is not obviously threatening and scientific. Chapter 1 looked at what ice balloons are, how to make them and some of the ideas that pre-school children have about them. I shall now explore the form these explorations can take and the sort of investigations they can lead to.

In explorations with ice balloons children need to have an opportunity to observe the balloon without any other resources. This is because they can be easily influenced by the resources you provide. An ice balloon on a table or in a water trough can promote enormous discussion and other resources can be introduced when the children appear to need them. There is no need to give magnifiers until the children have observed features that need magnification and there is no point in introducing thermometers if the children do not understand standard temperature measures and have not had the opportunity to measure the temperature qualitatively: to feel for themselves. From initial observations, the children will raise questions about the balloon, some of which can be further explored or investigated, and it is at this point that other resources can be provided to aid these investigations. With young children, further work has focused on questions which explore the concepts of materials, energy, forces and light:

(a) Materials: classification and description
    What is the outside of the ice balloon made of? What is the ice balloon itself made of? What does it feel like? What can you see? What does it look like? Why does the balloon split? What are the bubbles inside the balloon? How did they get there? Why is the balloon round? Why has it got a flat part? Why is the surface of the ice balloon misty?

(b) Energy: melting and solidifying
    Why does the ice melt? Does it melt quicker in water? Does it melt differently in water or air? Why does its shape change when it melts in water? Why does it melt quickly when salt is put on it? Why does it refreeze after the salt has been put on? Do the size and shape of the balloon make it melt quicker? Does it melt quicker if we touch it?

(c) Forces
    (i) Floating and sinking
        What happens when we put it in water? Does it float or sink in water? Does it float on the water or under the water? What happens if you push it under the water? Does it float the same way all the time? Can we change the way it floats? Can we make it sink?
    (ii) Friction
        Why does the ice balloon slide across the table? Does the ice balloon slide across other surfaces? Why does a paper towel stop it sliding? What happens to the ice balloon as it slides? Does sliding it make it melt quicker?
    (iii) Impact
        What happens when we drop the ice balloon in the water? What happens when we drop the ice balloon in the playground? Does the height of the drop matter?

(d) Light
    What can you see inside the balloon? Can you see through the balloon? How are coloured ice balloons made? What happens if you shine a torch through the balloon? Why can I see through some bits of the balloon and not others?

A group of reception and Year 1 children exploring ice balloons began with their initial observations.

It looks like a big ice cube.
Well, it looks like a balloon that one.

It's got plastic (*referring to the rubber of the balloon*).
It looks like spikes in there.
Looks like frozen glass.

As their observations became more systematic they used large magnifiers and began to see more detail:

There's a hole.
You can still see the spikes.
It's like frozen hair.

I then asked the children what they thought would happen to the ice balloons. A number of ideas emerged here and we were able to explore these further.

They'll break.
Melt if water goes on them.
If you throw them on the concrete floor outside they'll crack.
Me: Why do you think they will crack?
Because the concrete floor is harder than ice.

Relating her ideas to previous experiences, one child commented 'Glass breaks when it goes on the floor.' We then went outside and carefully threw one of the ice balloons across the playground to see what happened, and found that it did crack and shatter on the hard ground.

Later, in the classroom, one child said:

The sun will melt it.
Me: The sun will melt it? Is the sun shining on it here?
No.
Me: Will it stay like this all day?
No, it's going to shrink.
When the rain comes out it will melt.
It melts in water.
Me: Shall we try it and see?

We then got a tank of water and put the ice balloon in. This led to observations and discussions of how the balloon floated in the water.

It floats!
It's heavy! (*pushing it up and down and making it bob*).
The water's warm.
It's shrinking.
It's getting warmer.

It's slippy.
It's getting smaller now.

The children then hypothesized that the balloon in the tank would melt faster than the one on the table and so it was left in the tank while they focused on the other one. Later they noticed its change in shape.

Oo, it's like a bowl.
It's because it floated on the top.
That bit's in the water and that bit's out (*pointing*).

They took it out of the tank and looked closely at it and then they put it back in the water. It flipped over, so that the previously submerged part, which had melted quickly, was now above the water.

It looks like a big eye.
Look! It's gone sideways.

They seemed aware that it had melted faster under the water than above and related this to their observations about the water temperature. However, they did not seem able to hypothesize why it flipped over, and this could have been a focus for more detailed exploration.

I asked the children what would happen if we put salt on an ice balloon. They responded that it would melt:

Because it's salty.
Because it goes in.

An interesting hypothesis emerged. Lee began by saying 'In the winter, the sea on the ice . . . well ice . . . winter.' He was then interrupted by another child and later continued:

Well, I'll tell you about it. The sea that's at the seaside, well they used to be ice. The salt was in it. Then the ice melted into water and now it's salty water. Yeah it's going to make water in here.

This exploration gave the children opportunities to observe, to raise questions which could be explored further, to predict what was going to happen next and to formulate and communicate their hypotheses. The next step would be to help the children to plan investigations arising from these explorations. They could focus on how the ice melts in different situations, on the table, in water, outside, in a refrigerator over a period of time. They could look at the temperature of the ice as it melts, measured either qualitatively or quantitatively or both. They could explore what happens to ice in salty or plain water.

Other explorations could stem from collections. Collections which can be explored include rocks, plants, leaves, toys and musical instruments. Children can explore a collection of seeds such as a coconut, poppy seeds, bean seeds, etc. These could be seeds inside a collection of fruit from common examples, such as an apple, an orange and a blackberry, to more unusual ones, such as a kiwi fruit, a pomegranate and a mango. Having been given the collection, they can observe the similarities and differences between the fruiting bodies and/or seeds, notice their characteristics and begin to classify them according to observable features. In doing this, the children can be encouraged to raise questions which they can investigate:

- Will all the seeds grow?
- What do the seeds need to grow?
- Do big seeds grow into big plants and small seeds grow into small plants?
- What happens to the fruit/seed if we leave it?
- What part of the seed grows first/next?

Questioning by the teacher can also help formulate simple hypotheses:

- Why do you think the fruits are brightly coloured?
- Why do you think some seeds have got a hard shell?
- Why do you think the root grows first?
- Where do you think the seed gets its food from?

In such a situation, we can begin to find out about the children's ideas and this can enable us to assess their needs and plan activities which will be differentiated according to these needs. We need to remember that this only gives us a snapshot of the children's abilities within one context and as such the assessments we make must be tentative. We are able to indicate their abilities in a particular context, at a particular time, because of evidence we have collected through observation of and interaction with the children. This evidence will enable us to provide future explorations and investigations which will develop or challenge their ideas. In this way, exploration can be used to collect evidence to make informed assessments of the children's development.

A visit to a local shop or supermarket can lead to a vast number of explorations and investigations. During the visit, the children should have the opportunity to observe the different types of product on sale and how they are displayed, packaged and sold. Many shops are happy for children to visit the unseen parts of the shop and witness the different types of work involved. The children should actually buy some goods. This could lead to explorations back in school about the purchases. It may be decided to buy a collection of similar items, such as fresh fruit and vegetables, dairy produce, washing-up liquids, paper towels or biscuits. Back in school, observations and classifications of the produce can occur, according to different criteria such as colour, smell, composition and texture. Further research can later discover the country of origin, the cost per kilogram, etc. With a purchase of fresh fruit and vegetables, close observations can lead to pattern seeking and observational drawings, while explorations can look at whether they float or sink or whether they will grow. The fruit and vegetables can be used for printing or tasting or even in a fruit salad or a stew. Further follow-up work could involve recording favourite tastes in graphical form, designing some packaging for a delicate piece of fruit or a carrier bag for the supermarket, or looking at the recycling and decomposition of packaging. After purchasing different dairy produce, children could look at colour, taste and texture, with further research being carried out to find out how it is processed. Other activities can include using cream to make butter or cottage cheese, with investigations focusing on the time taken to make butter out of different types of cream or whether the processes are reversible or not. A collection of different washing-up liquids could look at observable differences between them (colour, thickness, smell) and proceed to exploring the lathers produced, their ability to make bubbles and the strength of those bubbles and to investigating their success in the removal of stains. This could be set in a familiar context of removing grease stains, food on plates or the staffroom coffee cups! Paper towels can be explored and investigated for absorbency, strength and efficiency. Biscuits can be explored for taste and flavour, texture, the way they crumble, with the science involved in baking biscuits or the biscuits' strength when dunked as resulting investigations.

The role of the teacher in explorations

Our final consideration concerns the difficulties or perceived difficulties of exploratory learning. In a busy classroom, with the need to meet ever increasing and changing demands from the curriculum, many teachers are using more prescriptive activities. This does not mean that exploration no longer has a part to play in the learning process. I believe that exploration enables us to cover more of the curriculum than prescriptive investigations. Exploration also develops the curriculum in a meaningful way. Exploration allows us to ascertain a child's conceptual needs and to plan specifically for these. With exploration, learning outcomes are more diverse and more closely matched to the children's needs and abilities. In the magnetism work, described earlier in this chapter, the original investigation was designed to focus specifically on which materials were 'magnetic' and which 'non-magnetic'. This rather narrow investigation would only match the needs of a limited number of children. The children who were involved in the investigation had a great many half-formed ideas which the investigation did not clarify, challenge or change. More open-ended exploration led to a wide variety of questions for further investigation, such as what thicknesses of material the magnets would work through, whether the magnet picked up all metals, and whether there are magnets of different strengths. The children began to challenge their existing ideas and formulate new ones.

In another example, children were asked to explore a range of objects connected to the concept of light. These included mirrors and other shiny objects, torches, lenses, old glasses, a kaleidoscope, in fact all the objects that could form part of an interactive display in the classroom on light. Free exploration of these objects led to questions being raised about the concept of light. When looking at her reflection in a spoon Donna asked 'Why is my face upside down this side but the right way here?' When using old glasses to look at writing Jason said 'I can make the writing bigger with these ones', and Jon noticed that the lenses 'felt different'. Kelly was fascinated by coloured glasses with which she looked at different colours, and this led to exploration using coloured sweet papers and later to an investigation to see what coloured felt-tip pens she could identify through different coloured wrappers. The initial exploration provided opportunities for differentiation by outcome and led to other activities which could be differentiated by task.

The organization of exploratory activities can be problematic. Although some people may feel that exploratory activities need little or no prior planning, this is definitely not the case. Planning needs to be very thorough to allow for every eventuality. In order to undertake any activity with children, we need to research the concepts and skills involved and consider our feelings and ideas. We then need to make plans so that every avenue will be covered. Even with thorough planning the unexpected avenues of enquiry can still occur, this creates opportunities for other explorations. This whole process requires some considerable degree of flexibility on the part of the teacher. A student recently described to me how the unexpected occurred during an exploration of plasticine and play dough with Key Stage 1 children. He had structured their explorations and in dropping the plasticine and play dough from different heights was hoping to lead on to planning an investigation to look more specifically at the forces involved. Unexpectedly the play dough bounced, and he was concerned that this was not only a deviation from his planning but also had detracted from his intention. It had, however, indicated his inflexibility and, although he soon realized the value of this unexpected exploratory avenue, he was momentarily concerned as to whether he should stick to his original plans or follow a new line of enquiry. On another occasion a student had abandoned all her fine plans for exploratory play activities and was undertaking more directed activities. This was because she was constrained by the enormity of her planning and convinced that she would not cover everything that had to be done.

In this way planning becomes a double-edged sword: we need to plan for every eventuality and to ensure that we have the knowledge to proceed down every avenue of enquiry, but we need to be flexible enough to move away from our plan if the unexpected happens and the learning resulting from that is considered to be beneficial. We know that we do not need to justify why we should abandon planned activities during the one snow shower of the year, so why should we feel the need to justify the desirability of following children's lines of enquiry?

If we do follow children's exploratory ideas, the role of the teacher, during exploration, will be crucial. The teacher's role, which will be discussed further in Chapter 5, should be to encourage, to challenge and to suggest, but not to dominate. Exploratory science activities may require more teacher input than prescriptive activities, but this can be justified by the increased learning involved.

The final difficulty of undertaking exploratory activities is concerned with the confidence of the teacher. Teachers need to have confidence that this approach to teaching and learning is justified by the learning outcomes. Such confidence will allow them to justify it to others, especially parents and governors who may wish to see evidence of the children's work. Teachers also need to have confidence to undertake activities with no apparent structure or organization and no predetermined ending. I use the word 'apparent' carefully here because exploration does not mean a lack of planning, organization or a predetermined ending. Rather, it implies planning and organization towards a number of predetermined endings, all within a recognized learning aim, and the flexibility to modify the planning and organization if that aim can be better met.

Summary

Exploration is important in the early development of scientific skills, knowledge and attitudes. It can be a useful tool

- in developing the skills of observing, raising questions, classifying, hypothesizing and communicating;
- in matching the conceptual needs and abilities of children and in planning differentiated activities to meet individual needs;
- in developing curiosity in children.

Teachers need to have confidence in exploration as an important part of the learning process of young children and to plan exploratory experiences in the classroom.

Useful reading

Lewis, M. (1992) Investigating ice balloons. *Primary Science Review*, 21: 12–13.
Ovens, P. (1987) Ice balloons. *Primary Science Review*, 3: 5–6.
Russell, T., Longen, K. and McGuigan, L. (1991) *Primary SPACE Research Report – Materials*. Liverpool: Liverpool University Press.

3

Seeking creativity in science activities

We should develop a creative teaching approach which challenges stereotyped views of science and, most importantly, clearly develops knowledge alongside skills. It is more important than ever to provide creative, stimulating activities in order to motivate children and assist the development of their scientific concepts, skills and attitudes. This can be difficult because children are often very demanding in their need for motivation.

Motivating children is possibly one of the biggest challenges teachers have to meet, and it does seem to be more and more important and more and more difficult to achieve. One of the reasons why stimulating science activities are necessary and difficult to provide is concerned with the incredible competition we face as teachers. Sophisticated television programmes and interactive books provide stimuli of a very high calibre. Interactive science centres are springing up all over Britain with resources that schools cannot possibly match. Computers, videos and compact discs are available in many homes, and children have access to a wide range of software, which they understand and which provides opportunities for them to experience the impossible – a trip through the solar system or a journey through a rainforest, for example. Shops sell a wide range of children's toys and science kits which cover all areas of science and enable children, for example, to experience electricity by making their own solar-powered toys, potato clocks or radios or to experience forces or energy through a variety of home-made toys. Changes in society with regard to employment, finances and household aids mean that children often have a larger number of adults and peers to interact with. As a result, children are immersed in science from an early age and by the time they arrive in school they will have had a large number of informal and formal science experiences and will have built up a large amount of tacit knowledge, as described in Chapter 1.

Today's children have plenty of resources, both human, paper, electronic and otherwise, to stimulate their senses. They have become dependent on sensory stimulation and are very critical of activities which are not motivating and exciting. Educational and organizational considerations provide a possible reason why stimulating science activities are difficult to deliver in the classroom context. It is a hard task to provide original, motivating ideas which enthuse the children, are manageable in the school context and have a valid and easily accessed teaching and learning point.

Scientific concepts, knowledge and skills are fairly unchanging and so it might seem that original science activities are almost impossible to deliver. We need to remember that while most science activities are 'old favourites' of ours, for many children they will be new experiences, and that creativity and originality apply not only to the activities we prepare for children to experience but also to our teaching. We can be original and creative in the provision of science activities, especially when we become confident ourselves in scientific understanding. Every teacher has the potential for originality and creativity, but too often we are constrained by our lack of science knowledge and a poor understanding of what science is and are unable to use our creativity in the classroom context. Primary teachers do not, generally, have a strong science background (School Curriculum and Assessment Authority (SCAA), 1994a) and have expressed concern about their abilities to cope with the 'higher levels of scientific knowledge required for work at Levels 3–5' (Department of Education and Science, 1991b: 31). We are also pressurized by the demands of an ever increasing curriculum which, with its accompanying assessment procedures, is 'too great to be manageable' (SCAA, 1994d: 1) and it is often difficult in the face of such demands to be original and creative. As a result, the planning and organization of creative science activities can appear daunting. If we are not successful in planning and organizational terms, we may suffer the effects of indiscipline and disorganization to the effect that learning aims will not be achieved, the class will be out of our control and the resulting chaos will be a threat to our sanity.

This is not a pretty scenario and one that we would want to avoid. However, the result of not providing creative activities can be disastrous in other ways, too. We may be perpetuating the traditional view of science and science education as a discipline which is boring, factual and difficult. We may have a peaceful classroom, but if we do not motivate the children they will view science in a negative way and this may influence them in their future learning. There have been concerns that enthusiasm for science is dwindling and that young people are not taking up science options at A level and university. If children are not motivated then it is sensible to conclude that learning will be impaired. The National Curriculum Council (NCC) recognized this when it said that 'pupils' attitudes affect the willingness of individuals to take part in certain activities' (NCC, 1989: A8). Harlen (1985; 1992) looks further at the part played by motivation in the learning process, arguing that if a learner is not motivated to learn then the learning potential is immaterial.

In the primary classroom it is recognized (DES, 1991b; Alexander *et al.*, 1992) that science teaching and learning have not only changed but improved since the 1988 Education Act gave every child, from five years of age, access to the curriculum. The rigour that the National Curriculum has brought to classroom planning has been received with some complaint that the curriculum is too prescriptive (Dearing, 1993), with little opportunity for originality and creativity. There are additional demands that science be taught as a separate subject to overcome the problems of curricular expertise (Alexander *et al.*, 1992). Alexander *et al.* (1992) have argued for a variety of organizational strategies and teaching techniques in order better to meet the differentiated needs of children, as a completely child-centred approach where every child is only taught as an individual 'is fraught with difficulties'. We should be careful not to assume that this is a mandate to resort to a more formal, didactic way of teaching, and we should also be careful that we do not omit parts of the curriculum because they do not match our views 'of how children's learning takes place' (SCAA, 1994b: 146).

Originality and creativity

What do we mean by 'originality' and 'creativity' in the provision of scientific activities? Originality and creativity are difficult to define because they have been taken to be synonymous (Childs, 1986) and because they are often used to mean different things in different contexts, for example art, technology and science. The dictionary definition of originality is concerned with the initiation of new ideas, design or style, while creativity is concerned with bringing into being or making something new. It can be argued that originality is the essence of creativity. There are disputes among psychologists as to whether creativity and originality are characteristics of the highly intelligent (Munn, 1966; Childs, 1986) or a potential in all of us which needs encouragement and motivation to flourish (Medawar, 1969). Harlen (1977a; 1977b) describes the progress of originality in children in terms of behaviours at various stages of development. This in part reflects the levels of subject competence for initial teacher training (Council for the Accreditation of Teacher Education (CATE), 1993). Teachers with little ability to provide original and creative science activities would have only a basic familiarity with the subject skills, concepts and knowledge and would have few ideas of their own. They would be dependent on others for ideas about what to teach and how to teach it. As teachers' subject competence increases and they become more knowledgeable about the skills, concepts and knowledge involved, they are able to extend or adapt ideas which are given to them. They may not be able to initiate original and creative activities but they will be able constructively to change them. The most original and creative providers of primary science activities would have an insight into the subject and an understanding of how to teach it. They would be able to 'exercise autonomy over approaches and resources' (CATE, 1993), producing novel ideas for teaching and learning.

They would also be enthusiastic about the subject and the teaching of that subject. Fraser and Tobin (1993) have identified features of exemplary Australian primary and secondary science teachers. These teachers were identified by asking other teachers, advisory staff and educators. Those nominated managed their classrooms effectively, used teaching strategies which focused on the children's understanding, provided learning environments which suited the children's learning preferences, had a strong content knowledge and encouraged children's involvement in classroom discussions and activities.

Encouraging and motivating children's scientific thinking

Providing different ways to package science ideas can help motivate children and encourage them to think about the science involved. We do not always have to provide 'hands-on' activities; we can promote discussion and thought in other ways. In my early years of teaching I would occasionally don a pointed hat and, waving my magic wand, tell my class of primary children that I was going to show them some magic. What followed was a series of 'magic tricks', all within a scientific theme. Once, focusing on forces, with the help of my magic wand I turned a cup of water, with a piece of card on top, upside down without spilling a drop; made a hard-boiled egg go into a bottle without touching or breaking it, made a small Lego diver drop to the bottom of a bottle of water and made a model person climb up some string. The children took great delight in explaining why I was not the world's greatest magician and why the 'tricks' worked. One child even said 'It isn't magic, it's science.' This was the most important part of this activity and provided the opportunity for the children to express their own ideas and actually challenged some of them. It was extremely important to explore the science behind each activity.

For the paper and cup 'trick' you fill a cup as full as possible with water and place a small piece of card over the top. When carefully turned over (Figure 3.1) the card remains over the opening and the water inside the cup. This is because the forces acting on the cup and card are balanced. If the downward forces are greater the water spills out of the cup. It is therefore advisable to

Figure 3.1 The paper and cup activity

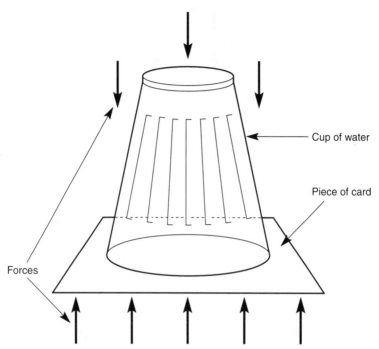

do this over a sink or bowl. Some children hypothesized that the cup was 'sticky' and that I had 'cheated'. Some children were able to identify the forces involved: 'It's the air pushing it up.' They did not really focus on all the forces involved, but as an activity to introduce forces it was motivating and challenging. I did advise them to try it out over a sink if they wanted to 'have a go' at home, and while I gather there were some wet tables, parents were generally pleased with the interest their children showed. I suppose this approach to science must have motivated the children because, years later, I would occasionally get young adults saying 'Do you remember when ... ?' Having fun was very important and motivating, but the most important part of the activity involved the explaining. It was essential to allow the children time to discuss their ideas; to draw conclusions about the science inherent in the activities; to interpret their findings and forward their conceptual development.

For the egg and bottle 'trick' you use a hard-boiled egg (shell

Figure 3.2   The egg and bottle activity

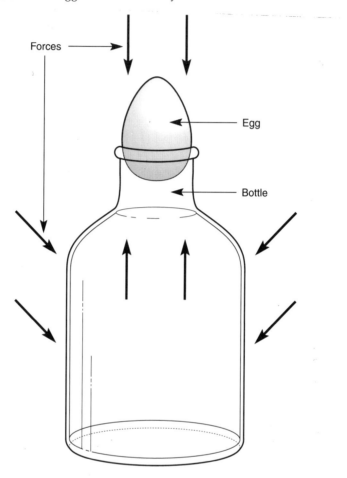

Forces

Egg

Bottle

removed) and a glass bottle with a wide neck. Check that the egg sits snugly in the opening of the bottle (Figure 3.2). Place a lighted match or taper in the bottle and put the egg back over the opening. The match or taper will go out and the egg will 'plop' into the bottle. As with the paper and cup activity, the underlying concept is forces. The egg should be only slightly bigger than the opening of the bottle, and it is forced into the bottle because the downward forces acting on the egg are greater than the upward forces. The balance of the forces changes when the air inside the bottle is heated and expands, escaping around the egg. As the air cools down the air pressure on the outside of the bottle is greater than on the inside and the egg is forced through the opening. The egg can be removed by increasing the pressure inside the bottle but it is easier to remove it manually. The children were fascinated by this display of 'magic' but the magician's guise did not fool them and they were convinced that there was a logical explanation and begin to look for it. I attempted to focus their discussions so that the forces involved were considered. Sometimes some misconceptions were highlighted; mainly the idea that some of the gas, usually the oxygen, had been used up, creating an unequal force. It was important that I did not encourage this misconception, and further follow-up work was needed to challenge these ideas. Children did not need to leave the activity with full understanding of the science involved, but it was important that they did not leave with misconceptions. Thought-provoking activities which make children think about the relevant concept are more likely to lead to later understanding.

The Lego diver activity is a version of the Cartesian diver. The Lego diver would have an upside-down test-tube attached to its back with a rubber band. The diver was then carefully inserted into a wide-necked plastic bottle full of water so that it floated, just under the water, at the top of the bottle (Figure 3.3). When the bottle was squeezed the diver would sink to the bottom of the bottle and when the pressure was released, would float back up to the top. After the initial excitement, the children would explore the diver for themselves; this would lead to some good observations being made and some simple hypotheses being developed.

Look! it works when I squeeze it.
The bubble gets smaller.

When asked why they thought the air bubble inside the test tube got smaller they responded:

The water pushes it up.
You are squashing the water inside.
It hasn't got much room when you squeeze it.

This could then be related to their experiences in the water trough and to ideas they had about floating and sinking. Usually

Figure 3.3   The Lego diver activity

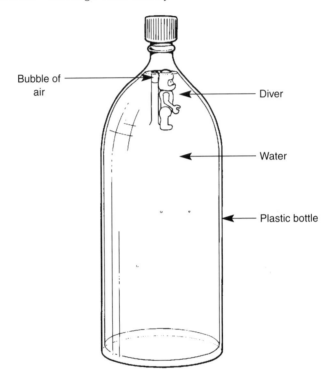

this consisted of the hypothesis that heavy things would sink and light things would float. Further investigation in the water trough could challenge this idea. This might include changing the shape of a ball of dough or plasticine so that it would alternately sink or float in the water, or taking a piece of aluminium foil and making it sink by squashing it up tightly.

For the climber activity, the climber needs to be made out of sturdy card and the shape should not be flimsy or have thin arms. Small pieces of drinking straws can be taped in place on the arms of the climber and string or strong cotton threaded through the straws. The top ends of the string should be fastened to a piece of card and the bottom ends weighted with plasticine (Figure 3.4). The children I worked with were able to make the climber climb up the string by holding the top of the model and rotating their wrist slightly. They were keen to make one for themselves, and in order to do so successfully they needed

Figure 3.4 The climber activity

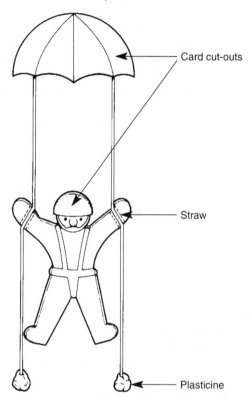

Card cut-outs

Straw

Plasticine

to explore the forces involved. There were two critical factors in making a successful climber, the first being the angle of the straws and the second being the weight of the plasticine. The straws need to be angled in for the person to climb up the string. If the straws were angled outwards the climber would not climb but would descend the string. This surprised the children, and they were then encouraged to examine why this happens. Closer examination allowed them to see that the straw should be angled in such a way so that with a movement of the wrist the straw becomes vertical and allows the string to drop through. The weight of the plasticine should be enough to allow the string to drop through the straw when the straw is vertical, but not so great as to affect the strength of the card or force the string through the straw. I have used this activity when exploring forces through a topic on Victorians. We explored a range of Victorian toys and looked at the forces involved and then made our 'climbers' in the shape of little chimney-sweep boys who climbed up the chimney. Once with Year 1 and 2 children we made Father Christmas climbers who climbed up to the roof. On another occasion Year 2 children designed their own 'climbers' and the resulting designs included an underwater diver who went down from a boat, a spiderman who climbed up to his web and a monkey who climbed up a tree. These excellent activities have also provided meaningful and creative links with both technology and history.

With each of these activities it has been most important to explore the science which underpins them. Without this underpinning the activity becomes educationally meaningless despite being creative and stimulating.

Visiting schools in England and other parts of the world has shown me the importance of stimulating, creative science activities which enthuse children and encourage them to investigate scientific phenomena in greater depth. I have witnessed some stimulating environments created in the classroom, bringing artefacts in, and taking children outside to provide more visually interactive displays to capture attention. In one Australian school I saw children working in a boat in the classroom and this was a motivating force and the children regarded it as a great privilege to work inside the boat. I applaud any motivating force which encourages the children in their work, but my main concern is that concepts, knowledge, skills and attitudes should be enhanced through these activities.

There are many science activities which appear creative and stimulating and the children appear absorbed, motivated and entertained but in many cases the actual scientific development occurring is small. Sometimes confusion occurs because a creative simulation or analogy is used. I have seen a potentially interesting science activity on the theme of Earth sciences which looked at volcanoes. A simulation of a volcano was achieved using jam tarts which when cooked behaved in a similar way to an erupting volcano. Those involved were having great fun and it was possible that the analogy between jam tarts and volcanoes was made explicit in some minds, but I was not convinced. In most minds the actual knowledge about volcanic eruptions and their geological links was not made explicit and the activity was 'fun' rather than developing scientific knowledge.

We need to take care that activities we use in school, while remaining creative and motivating and identifying the magic of science, illustrate a positive view of science and have a specific learning intention which remains at the centre of all teaching and which is at the forefront of any assessment. We need to provide positive science experiences for our children, but there does need to be an educational justification for 'entertaining science'. It is important but not enough to justify our planning on the basis that in today's society educational motivation appears to be of great importance in stimulating and encouraging scientific conceptual development. I would advocate creative science teaching, believing strongly that learning is enhanced by the provision of activities which are 'interesting and thought-provoking, and which can harness the child's natural curiosity and questioning' (Raper and Stringer, 1987: 20), but creative activities should emphasize the importance of a clearly identified learning intention. It is the ability to determine the learning intention and to plan for this which characterizes teaching as opposed to entertainment or child care. This theme is further developed in Chapter 5, but it is important that we stress here, in looking at creativity in science activities, the importance of learning through enjoyment and that enjoyable activities are not always synonymous with learning.

Creative science, information technology and the media

Children are often at ease with and stimulated by information technology (IT), while many teachers do not find it at all friendly. Bowell *et al.* (1994), in a pilot project concerned with the use of portable computers in school, reported that teachers had identified many positive outcomes from the regular use of computers in children's work. These included an increase in both the quality and quantity of written work, pupil effort, motivation and confidence. Children in primary schools today are growing up in a world of high technology and they do not seem to find the pace of change as confusing as adults do. Information technology can provide a stimulating way to develop scientific skills as well as scientific concepts and knowledge. Within the 1995 documentation for the National Curriculum (Department for Education

(DFE), 1995b: 1), the programme of study for IT identifies its cross-curricular nature and further identifies that IT capability involves the use of IT to solve problems and to support learning, and an understanding of the implications of IT in life and society. The Department for Education (DFE, 1995a: 1) endorses the development of children's IT capability in 'their study of science'.

There is a wide range of computer software and interactive videos which allow children to access scientific information and view scientific phenomena. The *Grolier Encyclopaedia* (published by Grolier Electronic Publishing), *Encarta* (Microsoft) and the *Dictionary of the Living World* (Media Design Interactive) are all available for CD-ROM use and contain a huge amount of data, some of which would be appropriate for Key Stage 1 children. Information technology can also encourage observational skills, provide help with children's planning and recording, assist in their investigations and provide opportunities for the interpretation of data. In this way IT can help to develop scientific skills as well as scientific knowledge in a motivating context. Observational skills and the ability to raise questions can be developed through the use of a good computer database program. This can help children to observe closely, to raise questions and to group according to observable features.

There are two types of database which can achieve this development: hierarchical databases, which compare one object to another by looking at a number of different attributes; and relational databases, which look at the relationship between objects, enabling children to group them according to observable features and begin to make and use simple keys. Some of these are closed or ready-made databases, which can be used to observe a specific group of things or which already contain data, while others are open and can be used to observe and classify a range of objects. They range from simple databases which are very suitable for Key Stage 1 children to complex databases which are more difficult to operate and contain a wide range of data. The *Information Handling Pack* (from the National Council for Educational Technology) contains programs such as Data Show, Notice Board, Our Facts, Branch and the Sorting Game.

Children do need to have experience of databases before using computer databases. It can be fun to map out a branch database on paper and then transfer it to a computer database. Children can start with a collection of fruit and begin to look for similarities and differences. They can begin to map out a simple branch database on paper by asking questions, the answers to which will differentiate the fruit. For example, given a banana, apple, pear, strawberry, kiwi fruit, avocado, star fruit, mango, pomegranate, grapefruit, orange, lemon, tomato and plum, the following questions can be asked:

- Is it yellow?
- Is it star-shaped?
- Does it have seeds?
- Does it have one seed?
- Has it got rough skin?
- Is it hairy?

The children will raise all these questions and many more. The database grows with each question in the same way as a tree grows up and branches out. The resulting database can look extremely complex (see Figure 3.5) but it can be as big or small as the children want. Young children who find writing difficult can still undertake the classification, as the databases do not have to include excessive writing. Pictures of the fruit or the actual fruit can replace the names and the questions can be written by older or more able children or the teacher. Older children will be able to make more complex databases with more branches and make more use of the written word. The use of the computer can make the procedure easier for young children. The computer will ask the children to write questions and name the fruit in each category. This can be done by more able children or the teacher or alternatively using a concept keyboard with pictures and questions on. The database grows quickly and can be added to by other groups of children at different times. As the computer takes you through each step you are not aware of the complexity of the database until a printout is made. Classification of some of the collections described in Chapter 2 can be made more fun in this way and can be as complex as the child or teacher wishes.

Computer simulations can provide opportunities to predict and hypothesize in scientific situations normally outside children's experiences. Some areas within the National Curriculum are difficult to develop in a practical way, that is through Attainment Target 1, Experimental and Investigative Science. For example, children need to develop skills in making predictions and

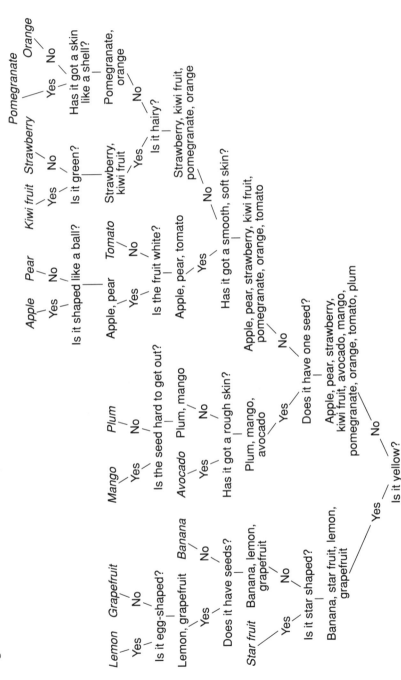

Figure 3.5 A branch database classifying a collection of fruit

hypotheses, and they should not attempt an investigation in science without having the opportunity to think about possible outcomes or to develop personal theories. They should then have the opportunity, where possible, to test out their ideas, but it can be difficult to give children these opportunities in every scientific situation. Within Attainment Target 2, Life Processes and Living Things, children are expected to study living things in their environment and develop an understanding that there are 'differences between local environments and that these affect which animals and plants are found there' (DFE, 1995a: 4). As they progress to Key Stage 2 they should begin to study the adaptation of plants and animals for their habitat and the feeding relationships within ecosystems.

In many schools it could be difficult to achieve this part of the National Curriculum in any meaningful way. It may be that the local environment holds limited potential for this type of activity; for example, it may be difficult to study aspects of rural ecosystems or classify wild flowers in an inner-city school. It may be more appropriate to study some plants and animals at a difficult or unseasonable time of year or when weather conditions are not suitable, or it may be that some activities would endanger animals and plants in the environment.

Some computer simulation programs can allow children to make decisions regarding the environment, predict the outcomes of their decisions and then test them out. Others can allow children to carry out observations which occur over a long period of time or may be regarded as environmentally unfriendly – the growth of a plant or the life cycle of a butterfly. Others can allow children to make difficult observations in a normal classroom context.

I do not suggest that computers can replace first-hand experience, that without any further input the children will develop the skills of predicting and hypothesizing, or even that the programs themselves will aid these developments without any teacher encouragement. However, IT can be a very useful tool to help the development of scientific skills in a motivating way (Table 3.1).

Information technology can also help to motivate children when planning investigations, modifying their plans as a result of discussions and trying them out in a practical way. This involves making both qualitative and quantitative measurements. I believe that Key Stage 1 children need to make qualitative observations

Table 3.1 How information technology can help the development of scientific knowledge, skills and attitudes

The advantages of using IT in science	*Considerations in the use of IT*
• Children find IT stimulating and motivating.	• Teachers often lack confidence in using new technology. IT can be frustrating if it is too complex for the learner.
• IT can develop the scientific skills of observation and raising questions through the use of databases and spreadsheets.	• IT cannot fully develop skills. Other work will always be necessary. Some databases and spreadsheets can be complex. The more sophisticated the software the more complex it may be to use.
• IT can develop the scientific skills of predicting and hypothesizing through the use of simulations and adventure games. They can enable children to make decisions and be practically involved in aspects of science for which this is difficult.	
• IT can develop the scientific skills of planning and investigating through the use of sensors and data-logging devices. This can allow children the opportunity to collect data at any time.	• Care needs to be taken in setting up the computer to avoid computer error which invalidates all data. Children's conceptual understanding will not be developed unless they are aware of what data they are collecting and why.
• IT can develop the scientific skills of measuring through a focus on qualitative observations and the use of sensors which measure accurately.	• Children need to have experience of making qualitative observations before they can understand the quantitative measurements taken with or without a computer.
• IT can develop the scientific skills of recording, communicating and interpreting through use of word-processing, database, and graphics packages, etc., which make recording of data more interesting and meaningful.	• Data recorded by means of IT will only be meaningful to children if they are allowed opportunities to consider and interpret them, and to communicate their interpretations to others.

- Children's conceptual development will occur through the choice of knowledge-based software.

- IT can aid conceptual development alongside the development of skills and attitudes. Conceptual development will only occur where children are given a variety of opportunities to work inside the concept.

---

before they are able to make sense of measurements taken using quantitative measuring devices. For example, children would need to explore the concepts of hot and cold in a qualitative way, that is by feeling water temperatures, in order to be able to conceptualize how temperature gauges, such as thermometers, work.

There are some computer data logging packages which can help Key Stage 1 children to take qualitative measurements and make their investigations fun. Data logging is the automatic recording, storing and displaying of information received from sensors which react to changes in temperature, light level, movement and so on. The sensors can be plugged directly into the computer or into an interface and can collect data in a digital or analogue form. Digital sensors are simple switches, such as pressure mats or light gates which register an on or off state, or trigger other events. Analogue sensors include temperature and light sensors which show a gradual change from minimum to maximum levels and can record changes over time. The PRISM software (National Council for Educational Technology) used in conjunction with 'Sense' data logging packages (Educational Electronics) can be appropriate for Key Stage 1 children, particularly when exploring temperature differences. When used for this purpose the computer screen shows the temperature of the sensors as colours. These sensors can also display temperatures digitally, which is easier for children to read than the scale on traditional thermometers.

The use of temperature sensors can motivate children to investigate more fully, but it is necessary to progress from qualitative data collection, either manually or on computer or both, before quantitative data can be understood. As already described, children would need to explore the concept of heat in a qualitative way, by feeling or by using simple electronic sensors which show changes by means of colour, in order successfully to interpret data collected using temperature gauges such as thermometers. They would need to have experience of both methods of data collection in order for analysis of data collected electronically to have any meaning for them. Another motivation for the use of sensors in simple investigations is that data can be collected over a period of time, and this means that children can collect data that they would not normally have access to or investigate for an extended period of time. Children could observe the temperature, light or noise levels in their classrooms over a period of time (Attainment Target 4) or how temperature or light affects the growth of seeds or plants over time (AT2). Using a remote sensor ('Sense and Control' from Educational Electronics) children can collect data away from the classroom and the computer, for example using a pressure mat they can explore how many birds visit a bird table (AT3), log the temperature, light and sound levels in the school garden over a 24-hour period (AT4) or the water temperature, air temperature, light and sound in the local swimming baths (AT4).

Recording and communicating are further important skills in science that can be developed in a motivating way through IT. They are also the part of a scientific activity that many children find a burden. How many times have you heard the plea 'Do we *have* to write about it?' The use of IT does reduce that burden for many children and makes the recording of data more exciting. Children can use cassette recorders to make audio tapes of their work in the form of a radio programme or a news flash. They can use video cameras to make a TV programme. They can use photographs of their work and make a book of their science activity or a photographic display. They can use computer programs to take the drudgery out of the writing up of scientific activities and make their records look more aesthetic and professional. Graphics programs allow children to draw pictures, make plans, graphs and diagrams. Word-processing packages can help children in writing and some can utilize a concept keyboard and are therefore of use with young children or children who find writing difficult. Written work can take a variety of forms – stories, poems, factual reports or the completion of cloze procedure (sentences provided with missing words which children have to enter in the appropriate place) or worksheets produced, by the teacher, using the computer. Stories and poems are a lovely cross-curricular way for children to record and communicate their feelings in science or their ideas on some areas of science. Word processing can also help in making the children's writing look professional and in giving children pride in their work.

Tables, plans, charts and graphs can be produced from data children collect, allowing them to record their results in an organized way. These may not always be appropriate for Key Stage 1 children as they do need physically to experience the graphical presentation of their data before feeding it into a computer. I have used simple programs to produce block graphs for Year 2 children, but have not found many programs which are suitable for graphical representation with younger children. Tables, plans and graphs can be used to develop interpretative skills. Graphs made during data logging in the classroom, using light, sound and temperature sensors, can tell you when the noisy and quiet times in the class are, what time it gets dark and when the teachers, caretaker and cleaners went home. Children can begin to look for patterns in the data or for anomalies such as:

- Who made the noise in the night?
- Was it a burglar or the hamster on a midnight prowl?
- What time does the boiler come on in the morning?
- Why does it get warmer in the classroom after 9.00 a.m.?
- Why is it noisy at 10.30 a.m. and 12.00 noon?

It is important that children have the opportunity to interpret their data and help to develop simple hypotheses.

Television and video are another useful motivating force for creative science activities. They can provide a stimulating introduction to a theme or concept, encourage and develop ideas during science work and suggest further explorations and investigations. Care is needed when using the media, as with all forms of IT and science educational books. We need to evaluate the educational worth of the programmes, ensure they are appropriate for the age of the children we teach, match our identified learning aim and fit in with our schemes of work. We cannot justify the use of programmes in isolation with little or no follow-up work or thought about the educational justification for using them. We cannot expect that a programme will do our work in planning, evaluating and assessing, and we cannot replace practical exploration and investigation with any programme, however good. We additionally need to be careful about the context of programmes. Some appear so full of razzmatazz that, while they are obviously motivating, the educational links are somewhat smothered; they may be so entertaining that the scientific point is lost. Others seem to perpetuate beliefs about science 'which arise from restricted and distorted understandings' (Harlen, 1992: 39); using the male, white, mad scientific inventor who is somehow alien to everyday life and people or provide images of science as factual, involving empirical methodology and being irrelevant to everyday life. We need to show children that science is applicable to us all, at any age, regardless of gender, race or ability, and that science is multifaceted, creative and can be qualitative.

Some creative science activities

'Difficult' scientific concepts can often be developed through creative, cross-curricular activities. In conjunction with a questioning approach, which encourages children to focus on the concepts involved and the skills we wish to develop, this can be very successful and help to facilitate the development of ideas and skills. A favourite of mine is to explore and investigate forces through art. There are a number of creative activities linking science and art which focus on forces. With each of these the recording is through art and the artistic result can be interpreted to focus on the forces involved. One activity investigates the patterns created by paint and sand pendulums. A paint pendulum can be made using a washing-up liquid bottle, with the bottom cut out (Figure 3.6). This can be hand-held or suspended upside down from a piece of wood bridging a gap between two tables and filled with either silver sand or liquid paint. When released the pendulum makes patterns on large sheets of paper. It is best to use dark-coloured paper for sand as it will show up better. The patterns created by different pendulums, different lengths of string and different methods of release can be investigated. While doing this children can be asked questions to encourage them to focus on the forces involved.

- What do you notice?
- How can you change the pattern?
- What do you think makes the pendulum start/stop swinging?
- When does the pendulum slow down?
- Why is the pattern different?

Figure 3.6 The paint pendulum

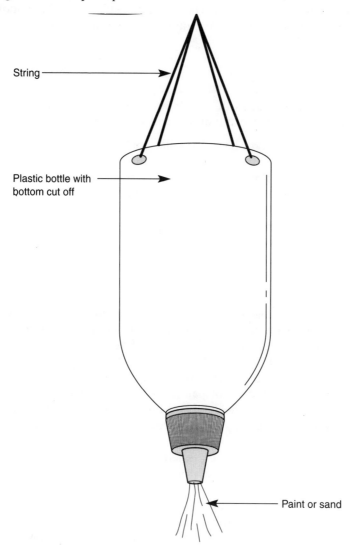

String

Plastic bottle with
bottom cut off

Paint or sand

It can be a messy activity, but small groups of young children can successfully look at the forces involved; the forces which make the pendulum start swinging, stop swinging, slow down, change the pattern and change direction.

The second creative activity involves exploring and investigating the effects of dropping ink, food colouring or coloured water from a pipette on to paper. The result is a 'splat'. If children look closely at these they notice a number of features about them.

Look, it's got spikes.
Mine's bigger.
This one's smoother.

The questions you ask the children can help to focus their ideas and lead to further explorations and investigations:

- How many spikes has your splat got?
- How can you make a splat with more spikes?
- Why do you think some splats are bigger than others?
- How can you make your splats bigger/smaller?
- What sort of splats do you think you will get if you let the drop fall from 1 metre/2 metres?
- What do you think makes a splat?
- Do you think your splat will look different if you use blotting paper/plastic/newspaper?
- Do you think the size of your drop will make a difference? How?

In this way further explorations can focus on the shape of the splats, the spikes coming out of the splats and how these change in number or size with height or size of drop, the type of paper or type of liquid used. In all cases the children should be encouraged to consider the forces involved in these changes; the force which makes the drop of paint fall, how changes in the force change the shape of the splat and how you can affect the forces by changing the paper, the way you drop the paint and so on.

The third creative activity I use to focus on forces involves a paint spinner. This can be a salad spinner with a circle of card inside it and a strip of card around its sides. You can also use a large circle of card fixed to an electric motor, placed inside a box (Figure 3.7) or with a salad spinner basket, with paper inside, attached to the base. There are available commercial paint spinners and these work in a similar way to a push-down toy spinning top. You could also use all three methods and, in addition to considering the forces involved, look at comparisons between the energy sources and how they work, as well as the end results. If the spinner has sides and/or a lid this is a relatively clean activity, although without the sides it can be messy and needs care and attention. Paint can be carefully put on to the circle and

Exploring the science in splats

the effects of centrifugal force can be seen in the resulting patterns. Children look carefully at the patterns resulting from the paint spinner and, once again, questions can focus on the forces and encourage them to explore further:

- Can you change the speed of the spinner?
- What do you think will happen if you use thicker/thinner paint?
- Do you think you will change the pattern if you use more/less paint?
- How do you think the pattern is made?
- Do you think the size/type of the paper makes a difference to the pattern?

This type of activity can develop some understanding of forces through consideration of what is making the paint drops move

Figure 3.7   The paint spinner

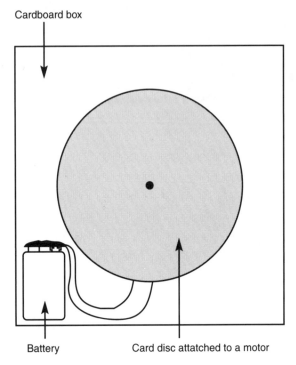

and make patterns, but will not develop full understanding of the forces involved. It is especially useful for developing understanding of the scientific process, allowing children to observe, predict, plan and hypothesize. All activities at this stage should be concerned with developing scientific skills and attitudes and with developing initial ideas about scientific phenomena which can be developed at a later stage. It is about experiencing and saying 'Wow look at that.' The 'wow' factor will be remembered at a later stage and better understanding of why will then begin.

The final activity looks at surface tension of water through marbling. This is an old activity used in many classrooms, although I would suggest that in most cases the science inherent in the activity is not focused upon. A few drops of oil-based ink are dropped on to a tray of water using a pipette. The oil and water do not mix and the oil floats on top of the water. Observations of the patterns on the water can lead to simple hypotheses.

Exploring the forces in a paint spinner

- Why do you think the ink is not mixing with the water?
- Why do you think the ink is floating on the water?
- What do you think holds the ink up?

The pattern can be captured by placing a piece of paper on top of the water and carefully lifting it off. The children can explore different colours, size of ink drops and type of paper. You can then observe what happens if you add a drop of liquid detergent to the water.

The difference between creative science activities and traditional science activities

I am sure that creative science activities can be found in many classrooms in many schools in many parts of the world. I have

Exploring floating and sinking through marbling

witnessed the creative simulations of Peter Jackson (1993a; 1993b), where creative, cross-curricular activities can be taught in an imaginative way which involves the 'whole human being' in purposeful activity. A classroom simulation on the Klondike goldrush (Jackson, 1993a) involved panning for gold and the Wakatipu kite festival (Jackson, 1993b: 24) involved making kites which are 'aesthetically pleasing ... fully steerable, have an adjustable harness and a colourful tail'. I have used similar types of creative activities in my own teaching, particularly when I have used literature as a starting point and re-created an imaginary situation in the classroom. *Stig of the Dump* by Clive King (1963), *The Selfish Giant* by Oscar Wilde (1978) and *Planet of the Monsters* by Stephen May (1985) have all provided the initial stimulus for Key Stage 1 work in science, mathematics, technology and English in a fun and motivating way. A cross-curricular day with PGCE students used *Jim and the Beanstalk* by Raymond Briggs (1970) to focus on work in mathematics and science. One set of activities involved making a wig for the giant which aimed to look at materials suitable for the hair, the adhesives used to glue the wig as well as size and shape and length. Another set of activities looked at light, lenses and vision in making a set of glasses for the giant. Providing a set of false teeth for the giant led to consideration of dental hygiene as well as materials suitable for making false teeth. The advantage of this type of working can be that the activity has obvious meaning to the children and they are more likely to be creative in their own right.

However, creative activities such as these may not be the norm. The recent SCAA (1994a; 1994b; 1994c) evaluation of implementation of science activities in the National Curriculum confirms my own analysis of school science made through visiting schools. According to SCAA, science activities in Key Stage 1 classrooms are mainly undertaken through small-group work accompanied by some whole-class teaching; 74 per cent of teachers used this method of organization in Year 1, 76 per cent in Year 2 and 69 per cent in Year 3 (SCAA, 1994c: 14). A smaller number of teachers (22 per cent in Year 1, 19 per cent in Year 2 and 25 per cent in Year 3) taught science mostly through whole-class activities accompanied by some small-group work. The children tend to be grouped according to age or ability, especially in vertically grouped classes, but ability is often determined by language and mathematical criteria rather than scientific criteria (SCAA, 1994c). Within the groups differentiation tends to be by outcome and not task, and children's individual learning needs are not necessarily taken into account.

The context of the science work is usually predetermined by the teacher who adopts a school policy to ensure coverage of the science curriculum. Most common at Key Stage 1 (between 37 per cent and 53 per cent) appears to be teaching to an 'agreed subset of Attainment Targets', although between 20 per cent and 30 per cent of teachers do not have identified coverage targets but attempt to cover as much as they can manage, with an additional 17 per cent to 22 per cent teaching whatever fits into their topic (SCAA, 1994a: 225). The research further shows a tension that exists between 'ensuring coverage and considering progress' (SCAA, 1994a: 92), and for many teachers, in my experience, the coverage of science content is becoming more important than the in-depth understanding of the concepts. The result could be a broad coverage of a large number of ill-defined ideas and some frustration on the part of learners who feel uncomfortable with their ideas and who find the subject demotivating.

The picture is emerging of a teacher who feels that his/her creativity is restricted by the demands of the National Curriculum and who provides activities which are teacher-initiated and teacher-directed, providing limited time for exploration and follow-up investigation resulting from the children's interests and needs. I am not arguing that teachers are not justified in being concerned about the coverage debate, or the best context for learning or how best to organize science activities, but I am arguing for continued support in developing creative science activities which address these concerns.

An example of a creative science activity can illustrate the main features of creative science. Exploring bubbles can start from a literature stimulus such as *Mrs Lather's Laundry* by Alan Ahlberg (1981) and can provide opportunities to look at everyday experiences in a different way. Children can use solutions of detergent to create bubbles of varying types. A variety of bubble wands, blowers and bubble-making devices can produce bubbles of different sizes and even bubbles of the same shape from different-shaped beginnings! Different types of washing-up liquid and bubble bath can be used to create the best, biggest, strongest, longest-lasting or most colourful bubbles.

Mrs Lather's laundry can be created in the classroom, and while the children can explore the bubbles, resulting in scientific development, they can also be involved in other curriculum development. Language development can occur through play interaction. Mathematical development can occur through the laundry's financial transactions and even historical explorations in researching how washing has changed through the years. An added stimulus could be a visit to a local laundry or dry cleaner, and this is likely to develop economic and industrial understanding (NCC, 1990) through exploration of the laundry as a workplace, the use of resources in the laundry and the disposal of laundry waste and the energy cost of laundry services.

From initial observations of bubbles, as part of Mrs Lather's laundry, children could explore light and colour, forces acting on the bubbles and different bubble solutions and water temperature. The resulting development in science could be in terms of the following concepts, knowledge, skills and attitudes, although I should stress that others could equally be developed. I should also add that it would be most unlikely that all these areas would be developed in one child through one activity.

Concept: Light
Knowledge:
- I can see that bubbles are coloured (light is made up of colours which can be seen in bubbles as a result of interference effects of light on the bubble film).
- I can see my own face in the bubble (light can be reflected in bubbles).
- I can see myself upside down and the right way up in the bubble (different surfaces of the bubble can result in different reflective images and you can see your image reflected in the concave and convex surfaces of the bubbles simultaneously).

Concept: Forces
Knowledge:
- When I blow bubbles, they fall to the ground, float away or burst (forces are acting on the bubbles).
- I can see the colours in the bubble swirling around (the forces acting on the bubbles can be seen in the swirling of the colours).
- My bubbles are always spherical whatever the shape of the bubble maker or wand.

Concept: Materials
Knowledge:
- I found out that different bubble mixtures produce bubbles of differing strengths, size and some can last longer.

Concept: Energy
Knowledge:
- I found out that warm water makes better bubbles (water temperature will affect quantity of the bubbles produced).

Skills
- Observation
  - I can see colours in my bubble.
  - The colours are swirling around.
  - Bubbles are always spherical.
- Raising questions
  - How big can I make a bubble?
  - What makes the biggest bubble?
  - How can I make my bubble stronger?
- Planning
  - How can I find out if the bubble mixture is stronger?
  - If I use a torch I think I will find out if the light goes through a bubble.

- Exploring and invest-igating
  - Which bubble solution is best for mak-ing bubbles?
  - What temperature is best for making bubbles?
- Predicting
  - What will happen if I blow a square bubble?
  - How long will this bubble last?
- Hypothesizing
  - Why are bubbles always spherical?
  - Why do bubbles burst?
- Communicating and interpreting
  - I can tell you which bubble solution is best.
  - I know why I can see my face in a bubble.

Attitudes
- Curiosity
  - I want to find out why the bubbles have different colours.
  - I am interested in how you can make a bubble last longer.
- Open-mindedness
  - I will try this and see what happens.
  - I think the bubbles may last longer because the mixture is thicker.
  - I thought this bubble would have more colours in but it has not.
- Critical reflection
  - I could make bubble mixture better by adding less water.
  - I could change my investigation to make it better.

So, what are the features of creative science activities? They can take a variety of different forms and have a number of different features. First, the context is likely to be novel and imaginative. A relevant contextual framework is considered to be an important aspect of effective science teaching (Association for Science Education, 1993) although this can be achieved through either a topic or subject-specific method. This may involve creating a whole environment in which to work such as a whole-class simulation or immersion in a theme or book. It may involve using a ready-made environment such as computer simulation. It may involve the creative use of resources or technology, such as use of the computer to add a dimension to an investigation. It may involve using or looking at everyday phenomena from a different perspective, such as looking at splats or magic tricks.

Second, the work is likely to be cross-curricular in nature. This has the advantage of making the activity meaningful by not separating the curriculum or knowledge into discrete compartments which bear little relation to the outside world. In conjunction with a suitable context this provides clarity of meaning for the children involved. The activity will involve the whole child in a meaningful way and this will improve motivation for learning in general.

Third, the work is likely to be more exploratory and take into account the children's own ideas for further development, modification or change. In this way it will develop skills, concepts, knowledge and attitudes in a coherent way. It will probably cover a larger number of areas of development, as described in the example of Mrs Lather's laundry, and be better differentiated to meet children's individual needs.

Fourth, the activities are likely to be pupil-generated to a larger degree. Teacher support and guidance are necessary for success, but not teacher dependence. From an initial stimulus and through the provision of resources, which the children can use to explore and raise questions, simple investigations can be planned by the children to answer their questions.

There is a need to be well planned to enable the children to follow their own investigative pathways, but there is also a need to be flexible to allow new and unforeseen pathways to be explored. In exploring and investigating bubbles the teacher or the children may choose to explore the concepts of light, materials, forces or energy, developing knowledge in the ways described earlier, but it is equally possible that other unexpected concepts and knowledge will be explored. I have often been amazed by the ingenuity of learners in looking at something old from a completely new perspective. I have discovered this most often when exploring ice balloons, where new areas for exploration are uncovered each time I teach it. The added advantage of this is that teaching remains exciting and innovative and I remain enthusiastic despite visiting an activity on numerous occasions. There are issues here related to the teacher's role in decision-making about curriculum organization and teaching strategies, and these will be further explored in Chapter 5.

More traditional activities differ in a number of ways. They are more likely to be initiated and directed by the teacher, to consider only one small aspect of science, to relate only to the science curriculum, to have a limited time-span and to be less well matched to the differentiated needs of the child. I am not advocating teaching solely through creative science activities; neither am I suggesting that more traditional teacher-initiated and structured activities cannot be creative in their own way. A balance in the provision of activities is always desirable and is more likely to achieve quality learning. I am also not suggesting that creative science activities as described in this chapter are not themselves without problems.

The dangers of creative science activities

The difficulties teachers face in providing creative science activities need to be identified and considered in order for teachers to make informed decisions as to whether to provide such activities at all or whether to proceed with caution. In many ways the way to evaluate creative science is to 'have a go and see', and there is little anyone can do to replace first-hand evaluation. However, it is an advantage for teachers to know the dangers before they embark on what may be a new venture. Some of the dangers of creative science have already been discussed earlier in this chapter but warrant further consideration.

Organizational difficulties were discussed in the early parts of the chapter and are recognized to be a major obstacle in the path of creativity. We obviously want our children to have quality experiences but we do not wish to provide stimulating science activities at the expense of quality learning or classroom sanity. We want our children to have exciting experiences but not to disregard individual safety. We want to enjoy our teaching and learning experiences but we do wish to consider the needs of others in school: other classes, teaching staff, the cleaning staff and the caretaker. Whole-class simulations and literature-based explorations can pose organizational difficulties, but not all creative science activities have to be as adventurous. Smaller-scale activities, small-group work and activities which are partially structured to provide quality teaching and learning opportunities can be a good start, and ensure a smooth-running but enjoyable classroom environment. Cumming (1995) succeeded in providing a stimulating set of experiences for her class of reception and Year 1 children through the theme of Humpty Dumpty. Her activities were, in the main, teacher-initiated and included looking at forces in the structure and shape of eggs, looking at materials through the cooking of eggs and growth by using egg shells to grow seeds. I have used 'Hickory Dickory Dock' in a similar way, providing structure in my organization. As our teaching confidence develops we can attempt more experiential ways of learning but still retain the structure and support we need.

The debate as to whether creative science activities which are cross-curricular in nature can provide effective coverage of the National Curriculum will remain with us for some considerable time to come. As Harlen (1993: 2) said in an editorial for *Primary Science Review*, 'teaching methods and organisation are never static', and any advice as to whether we organize our teaching in a cross-curricular way, how we group our children and whether class or individual teaching is more effective is both confusing and contradictory. Harlen (1993: 2) continues by stating that we should be careful to avoid 'moving to the extreme where, to avoid the complexity of addressing the curriculum through topics (which relate the children's understanding to real experience), we replace it by the simplicity of teaching to the statements of attainment'.

We can be creative in the provision of science activities using a variety of teaching and learning methods. Creative science does not have to be cross-curricular but it does need to be satisfying for the children and teachers involved. I hope that the arguments already set out in this chapter make the point that curriculum coverage can be obtained through creative exploration, but the difficulty remains of monitoring for the diversity in coverage of creative, flexible activities. Additionally, forward planning can be disrupted as children move along unexpected avenues. The solution is not 'to put all your eggs in one basket' but to plan a variety of creative teaching methods, some of which allow children to take more responsibility for their own learning while others are structured to provide the experiences we know they need to fulfil the National Curriculum demands and their own development. In this way the monitoring of learning becomes no more complex than it is in any other classroom environment.

Assessment of learning can be another difficulty that teachers face. It is especially so if we allow assessment to drive the curriculum rather than use assessment to inform us of the children's needs and to help in planning differentiated activities. If we become so focused on summative assessments, the result will be an arid curriculum with little creativity and poor motivation and development on the part of the children. In the creative classroom assessment can still take place, and we can hopefully move away from assessing the work children have undertaken to assessing the individual achievements of children. Assessment as an individual process becomes no more difficult in a creative activity than it does in any other activity. Remember, though, that assessment should not be allowed to determine teaching but should support it.

What may be more of a problem is the actual learning which occurs. Creative science does not mean that we do not assess the children's needs and plan accordingly. Neither does it mean that we should not have specific learning objectives which we set out to achieve. It does mean that we need to be more skilful in facilitating children's learning. We need to ensure that there is some real learning involved in the activity and not simply a fun set of experiences for children. I have seen classroom activities judged on the basis of the fun element rather than the learning element. Learning should be fun, it should be motivating, it should be creative, but it should also be meaningful. The role of a teacher implies identifying the learning inherent in an activity and assessing its development.

The final problem with creative science is concerned with the message about science that we are projecting. We want children to realize that science is fun and creative, but we also want children to get a full picture of the nature of science. We do not want science to appear completely serious, and irrelevant to everyday life, but neither do we want it to be considered frivolous. In planning science activities, we do need to be careful about the messages that we are giving to children about the nature of science and ensure that they have a balanced picture. If we provide relevant, meaningful and motivating experiences for children they will have fun and develop the desire to understand the scientific principles underpinning the experiences.

Summary

- Good science teaching can be fun and effective and creative science can be a reality.

- Creative science activities can take a variety of forms. No one way is better at everything than another.
- Creative science explorations can be very effective at developing the whole child in a coherent, cross-curricular way.
- While creative science activities are enjoyable and entertaining it is important to remember the learning objectives involved.
- In planning creative science explorations there is a need to consider the messages about science we are conveying.

Useful reading

Ovens, P. (1987) Ice balloons. *Primary Science Review*, 3: 5–6.
Smith, R. (1990) Stories from science. *Primary Science Review*, 13: 4–5.

4

Developing positive attitudes in science

The area of attitudes is complex and it overlaps with all aspects of life. An attitude can be described as a 'posture or position that is adopted' or an 'expression of a view or thought' (*Chambers Twentieth Century Dictionary*). Attitudes can usually be observed in some kind of behaviour and the importance of the resulting behaviours is thought to affect performance in science (Harlen, 1977a; 1977b; 1985; 1992; Raper and Stringer, 1987; National Curriculum Council 1989). The development of scientific attitudes has been an important part of school science for many years. The early development of the National Curriculum acknowledged the importance of scientific attitudes (Department of Education and Science (DES), 1987) but identified difficulties in their assessment (DES, 1987; 1988). The result was that in the eyes of many teachers attitudes were devalued. If we do not have to assess them, why should we develop them? Their recognition in the non-statutory guidance (NCC, 1989) does little to redress the balance. Changes to the curriculum (Dearing, 1993; Department for Education (DFE), 1995a), together with concerns about curriculum coverage, already discussed in Chapter 3, seem unlikely to improve the development of attitudes in school science. Arguments for the development of attitudes are twofold: that we should be developing the whole child and that the development of positive attitudes is likely to have an important effect on the development of scientific concepts, knowledge and skills. In considering the development of positive attitudes we need to be aware that there are two important types of attitude related to science – attitudes *in* science and attitudes *to* science – and that, while their development is of equal importance, they are quite different.

Attitudes in science

There are a number of attitudes which we should develop as part of the education process, and some of these are particularly important in science teaching and learning. These attitudes can be assigned broad groupings and there is some overlap between them (Figure 4.1).

Many of the attitudes we would wish to develop in children are useful to other areas of learning as well as later in life. We would wish children to be cooperative, tolerant, flexible and sensitive in many aspects of their education and wider learning outside school. The young egocentric child described in Chapter 1 will not readily be cooperative or flexible. Indeed, the development of these attitudes is similar to the development of concepts and skills, in that it is a long process. As with skills and concepts we need to have an overview of the attitudes needed for successful development and we need to work continually towards the development of those attitudes. Children in our care will not develop fully in this area but our teaching should provide the foundations for the development of positive attitudes throughout their future lives.

Motivating attitudes

These are the attitudes which are necessary in the initiation of an exploration. The need for a motivating force, a stimulus or an enthusiasm was discussed in Chapter 3, while Chapter 2 considered how explorations could develop curiosity. I think it is enough here to reinforce the need for children to want to learn.

Figure 4.1 Attitudes in science

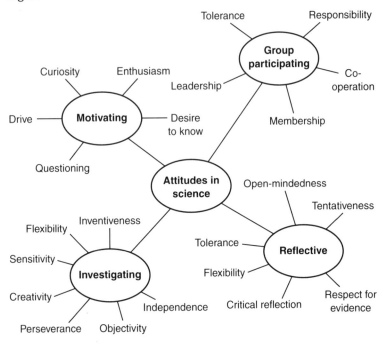

Without the drive to want to find out or know about something, teaching becomes an impossible task.

As teachers we have an important role in encouraging children's explorations, and in order to be successful in this we need to understand how a child develops the desire to learn. All children show some curiosity and, if encouraged, this will develop into a motivation to learn about the world around them. Sometimes this curiosity is discouraged, particularly where it could lead the child into danger. The present generation of children have fewer opportunities to be adventurous than previous generations. This is connected to the complexities and dangers of today's society. As a young child I was not particularly adventurous, but spent a great deal of time exploring my environment and discovering the delights of the local woods, waste land and building sites and, in doing so, developed scientific knowledge which was useful in my future life. Today children's lives are more structured. Parents today generally do not consider it safe for young children to frequent building sites; we are concerned about the safety of our children when 'playing out' and we tend to keep a much closer eye on our children than parents of former years. In some respects, children have paid for this greater care and have fewer opportunities for free play and exploration. While this picture of middle-class life does not ring true for all of the children of today, the basic tenet remains that children have less opportunity for developing curiosity. For many children the instinctive need to find out is thwarted because it is not always convenient to have a child constantly asking questions, touching things and enquiring. Take a class full of inquisitive five-year-old children and it is necessary to channel their inquisitiveness, not only because of safety but because they should learn to consider the needs of others.

Learning that they are not the centre of the universe is a hard lesson for all children to learn and the consequences are often that their desire to find out, to learn, is damaged. Donaldson (1978) describes this in terms of a tension between wanting to know and the process of finding out. Very young children have no ability to see the consequences of their actions, and as the ability to think inwardly about actions develops and children are able to deduce from inference what will happen, they will often appear less curious even if they are not less curious. Their decision not to find out may be based on experience: 'I won't explore the pond because I've fallen in three times or because my parents have told me off three times.' It may be that they decide not to explore because they expect a certain outcome, even if it is not based on experience. They may have been told something will happen or be able to imagine it happening. Children who will not go near a snake have probably not been bitten by one; they may not have been told that snakes bite, but they have developed their ideas from a variety of sources which will influence their curiosity about snakes. At one time, my son was terrified of fireworks. He was convinced that one would land on his head. This was not because one had hurt him or because he had been told they would land on his head, but because he deduced 'that what goes up must come down and it will probably be on my head'.

We need to harness natural curiosity and help children to develop the desire to learn within the parameters we set them, and this is where other attitudes overlap with curiosity.

Group participating attitudes

Children need to consider the needs and safety of others. Within their families they soon learn that other children and adults have needs and rights. When they mix with larger numbers of children in play schools, nurseries and at school, this need to consider others becomes more important. They cannot rush around and explore everything they want, when they want. They have to conform to school rules. Sometimes this is difficult for children and it creates a conflict between school and the child. In the worst situation alienation occurs and children resent having to be at school and having to conform.

In scientific explorations we often want children to work with others; we normally group our class activities so that children work in small groups (School Curriculum and Assessment Authority, 1994c). We should be aware that sometimes children 'learn more efficiently when working individually rather than with others' (Harlen, 1977b: 27), but that the sharing of ideas and efforts can provide very effective learning opportunities and should be encouraged where appropriate. However, we need fully to consider the attitudes and skills needed for effective group participation. I am not convinced that we, as adults, are particularly good at group work. If this is so, then it becomes all the more important that we consider what attitudes and skills are needed and plan how these can be developed in both ourselves and those we teach.

In order to work effectively as a group children need to co-operate with each other. Cooperation should occur regardless of the group's members – whether the group is based on friendship, gender, ability or any other criteria. Teachers will attempt to group children according to different criteria or allow them to group themselves, but the long-term aim must be to enable children to work in any group regardless of the group constitution. Children who are fully cooperative in a group situation will be responsive to the needs of others in the group, will try to accommodate the ideas of others and will settle group difficulties without resorting to argument or appeal to the teacher. Young children are not naturally cooperative. They tend to work independently in group situations. They are often reluctant to share resources or ideas with others and the group may need constant supervision to avoid disputes occurring. The class teacher may need to lay down a set of rules for working in groups and will then need to wean children off teacher support and encourage them to make up their own rules for working. For this to occur there needs to be adequate time provided to allow the children to 'sort themselves out', to make group decisions, and this should be built into any working plans.

When working in group situations children need to be tolerant towards other group members. They need to consider the needs of all the group and respect the ideas of others. This may mean initially selecting groups which are able to cooperate with each other. These groups should not remain static. Membership and roles (coordinating the group, recording decisions, and so on) should change from time to time to enable children to learn and display scientific attitudes in a variety of situations.

Working in groups makes science activities organizationally easier than individual work, but in many instances children at this age work individually within a group. I observed one mixed group of children who were working together, in a competitive situation, making paper aeroplanes. The task was to make an aeroplane which would fly over 10 metres. For each aeroplane which achieved this the team would get a point. The group divided into gender groups, with the boys quickly making successful aeroplanes but not wishing to help the girls, who were uncertain how to design an aeroplane. The fact that the girls' inability to make a successful aeroplane would mean fewer points for the whole team was immaterial! Even with young children gender issues play an important part in inhibiting good attitudes for group participation. It is clear that, whatever the group constitution, cooperation is not a natural part of human behaviour. Team work in adults is often little better. We can democratically make decisions, but individuals often interpret these differently or ignore them and follow their own course. If we do not always see attitudes for group participation in older children and even in adults, it is very unlikely that Key Stage 1 children will exhibit better-developed attitudes. These attitudes need to be continually encouraged, throughout the learning process, in order for their development to be successful.

Mixed-ability grouping can also cause difficulties in investigations. These groups often consist of individuals with different attitudes in and attitudes to science, as well as different abilities (Johnston, 1992). In such instances the investigation can enhance rather than dissipate anxieties. This is because more advanced learners can be so enthused with their own hypotheses that the insecure are carried along and do not have the opportunity to explore their ideas and develop at their own rate. Sometimes co-operation and competition become confused, as it did with the group of children described earlier.

Children have all experienced being compared to others, even before they come to school, and they quite easily interpret what we consider to be cooperation to mean competition. Some children are so anxious not to fail that they will not compete or even cooperate. As Harlen (1977 b) says, failure means frustration and unhappiness, and success in a competitive situation is not available to all.

Responsibility is another important attitude for both individual and group work. Children who take full responsibility for their learning are able to work independently, without constant supervision, and will attempt to overcome problems they face without teacher help. Young children will need considerable help to reach this stage in their development as it presupposes a maturity and experience lacking in young children (Harlen, 1977b), but with help and guidance they can begin to play a more responsible part in their own learning. Harlen (1977 b) identifies a close relationship between the development of responsibility and cognitive development. This does not mean that we can expect responsibility to develop without opportunity. We need to provide children with a framework in which they can take responsibility for their own development and also to provide time for them to make decisions for themselves and resolve any difficulties. They should develop the understanding that they are responsible for their own actions. It is a natural human reaction to rationalize why things do not go according to plan but it is not enough to deny responsibility because intention is absent. Steven, a Year 2 child, had a wonderful experience exploring materials but there was considerable mess on the floor. When asked to tidy it up he responded 'It's not my fault, I didn't mean to.' This kind of response is becoming more apparent in all ages of learners, from children through to adults, and we need to develop the idea that responsibility does not mean blame and that we can be responsible for our scientific explorations without blame when things go wrong. Without this knowledge children are unlikely to want to be either responsible or inventive as it could lead to trouble.

We would want all children to develop attitudes to assist group participation – cooperation, tolerance, responsibility and leadership – but we should remember that they do not exist naturally. We should also remember that being a member of a group is not easy for children and should attempt to develop these attitudes in a coherent way.

Investigating attitudes

There are some important attitudes necessary, or desirable, for effective engagement in an exploration or investigation. We have already discussed the importance of creativity in the provision of science activities. Creativity is also important for children in their explorations. This comes as a surprise to some teachers, because their image of science is not compatible with the notion of creativity. The National Curriculum non-statutory guidance identifies the importance of creativity and inventiveness (NCC, 1989), but there is little guidance on how we develop children's creativity. Children learn from us what aspects we value and, in many cases, creativity in science is not one of them. We need to remember that creative scientists are the key to the future, and we should encourage all our future scientists in their creativity.

Within the scientific process children also need to exhibit flexibility and independence. This is different from flexibility of thought, which will be discussed later in the chapter. Flexibility in the process of science involves children in being prepared to modify or abandon their line of exploration or investigation because a more fruitful one emerges. This flexibility is also an essential ingredient in working with others in an exploration as children need to be flexible enough to encompass the views of others. Independence involves children in having ideas of their own about the exploration they are involved in. The development of independence involves children in moving away from the automatic acceptance of others' ideas and being able to make decisions for themselves. These decisions should be based on all the available evidence and not be made just because someone else has a similar idea. Children need to have the confidence, responsibility and independence to explore and investigate in and beyond the classroom, and to use other sources of information such as outside agencies and experts (Raper and Stringer, 1987).

While exploring and investigating, children need perseverance. They should not give up at the first attempt if something does not succeed. Early perseverance in children can be described as 'the tendency to continue an activity or task once it has begun, despite difficulties or lack of immediate success' (Harlen, 1977a: 36). We all recognize the young child who says 'I can't do it', having made little or no attempt at the task. As children develop they are more likely to persevere with activities regardless of the effort involved providing there is a reasonable chance of success. They are also more likely to try other ways of working in order to achieve a successful result. The types of activity we give to children and the way we structure activities can help to develop perseverance in children. Activities should not be so difficult that children cannot see a way forward and give up. Children need to feel a degree of success and a sense of achievement in order to motivate them further. When they do encounter difficulties in their explorations they need help in identifying the way forward and encouragement to persevere.

Objectivity is necessary in order for children to identify variables and undertake fair testing. Raper and Stringer (1987) believe that fair testing will help to develop both objectivity and honesty. This can be achieved by encouraging children to examine their ideas and practice and valuing their failures as stepping-stones to success. Objectivity is a very important attitude in science because without it the development of scientific skills, concepts and knowledge is impaired. Objectivity is implicit in many parts of the scientific process. It is the basis of fair testing and, as described in Chapter 2, it can be developed through explorations. Successful interpretation of data requires a degree of objectivity to enable unbiased interpretations to occur.

Within an exploration or investigation sensitivity towards others is necessary. This includes sensitivity towards the views and abilities of other children but also sensitivity towards, and a responsibility for, all living things in the environment. 'Unless investigation and exploration are governed by an attitude of respect for the environment and a willingness to care appropriately for the living things in it, such activities could result in unnecessary interference or unpleasant harm' (Harlen, 1985: 50). These attitudes develop mainly through example. Good examples come from teachers who develop an understanding of the world around them by observing animals and plants in their natural environment or creating suitable environments in the classroom. It is possible to study plants and animals in the school, but we need to be careful that we understand all the needs of those plants and animals to enable us to care adequately for them. We should not collect plants and animals and study them in school unless we are able to return them to their natural environment later. If we collect frog spawn from a local pond and neglect the needs of the developing frogs the result will be a smelly, messy death for the animals concerned, and children will not pick up the right messages about the importance of living things.

We also need to be careful that we do not encourage anthropomorphism. Animals and plants have different needs than ours, and we cannot assign human values when dealing with them. What is considered bliss for a wood-louse, rotting wood, vegetation and darkness, is considered abhorrent to us. I have been involved in creating wildlife areas within school where children can attract butterflies, explore pond life and grow wild flowers. I have also provided a safe environment for other animals to live in school. At one school we kept rabbits in a school quad, where they could roam freely during the day and be observed and cared for by the children. We also used an incubator to hatch ducklings who later went to live at another teacher's home. The development of understanding and sensitivity towards living things engendered by these activities was great. On another occasion children were involved in planting trees and shrubs on some waste land. In doing this they developed an understanding of the need for these plants, both aesthetically and physically. In taking responsibility for the planting the children were also less likely to destroy the trees and shrubs at a later date and to dissuade others from doing so.

We can also provide a good example by the way in which we conduct ourselves inside or outside the classroom. Swatting flies and ignoring litter are bad examples. Releasing flies and spiders back into the outside world and picking up litter are good examples. One teacher I know always carries a plastic bag around with her to pick up any pieces of litter left by others. This has had an effect on children around her who become much more aware of the mess around them and more willing to dispose of not only their own waste but also of others' waste.

Reflective attitudes

In undertaking an exploration or investigation children need to develop reflective attitudes. These are attitudes which help them objectively to consider their data, interpret evidence and make tentative hypotheses, but remain flexible enough to change their ideas if they are not consistent with the evidence. Children need to embark on a scientific activity with an open mind; this involves considering the views of others but not, of course, total acceptance of others' ideas without due consideration of their own. Young children will often have firm ideas about phenomena based on their own experience, but because their experiences are limited their ideas may be unsophisticated. They may also, in some cases, be so firmly held that they inhibit the process of exploration and investigation (Driver, 1983).

Ideas, while firmly held, may also be hidden. This may be because the ideas of others, particularly the teacher, are respected and are not contradicted. This indicates some degree of tolerance on the children's part, and while we would wish them to tolerate the ideas and interpretations of others they do need to have the ability and confidence to challenge ideas and interpretations if they do not match their own. In some respects children seem able to allow two contradictory ideas to exist together and often do not appear to recognize that they are contradictory (Driver *et al.*, 1985).

Having obtained evidence which either confirms or contradicts their ideas, children then need to have respect for that evidence. Harlen (1992: 42) identifies respect for evidence as 'being central to scientific activity'. Respecting evidence implies that the children are not biased in their interpretations because of existing ideas. They need to realize that if the evidence does not match their ideas and expectations they may challenge the evidence but not ignore it. They still need to respect valid interpretations based on the evidence which are not compatible with their ideas and expectations. There is an element of tentativeness involved in respecting evidence. Children need to see that all evidence is tentative, that they can only draw conclusions with supporting evidence, and that, even then, the conclusions may be subject to challenge.

Children also need to be flexible enough to change their ideas in the light of evidence or to review procedures critically (Harlen and Jelly, 1989). Flexibility involves a recognition that there may be other ways of looking at evidence, a willingness to consider evidence from alternative viewpoints and to change ideas in the light of evidence. To reflect critically on a scientific exploration or investigation involves a willingness to consider alternative ways of undertaking an investigation to improve the outcome – to evaluate procedure. This often involves consideration of how an investigation was best suited to answer questions raised during initial exploration. It could involve consideration of the planning of an investigation or how 'fair' the investigation was. As Harlen (1992) has indicated, this is a mature activity and young children find it difficult. Sharing ideas, planning and interpretations helps to identify different perspectives and has the initial advantage of giving children access to the ideas of others. Development of group cooperation skills and consideration for others assist in the further development of these attitudes.

The development of all attitudes in science is a long process. Like the development of skills and concepts, children will progress at a rate compatible with their abilities. The analogy with building a wall is apt. The final wall is our aim and although we may only lay a few bricks we need to understand the final wall plan, know what mix of cement to use and what size bricks are best. In the development of young children we only lay a few bricks, but they are the foundation for a wall which will be very robust. We need to have a clear idea of children's developmental needs and how they might progress. We need to know what scientific attitudes are necessary for children to develop and how those attitudes can be developed. This knowledge will enable us to assist children's development effectively.

The development of attitudes in the classroom

A class of young children engaged in scientific exploration and investigation of 'air' illustrated for me the complex nature of attitude development and the many influences on it. These children were involved in exploring a range of scientific ideas including the idea that air had weight. This idea had been introduced to them and they had accepted it and were undertaking explorations and investigations to illustrate it. They were working in small groups and were extremely motivated, enthusiastically debating ideas and questioning each other about their

Figure 4.2   Investigating whether air has weight

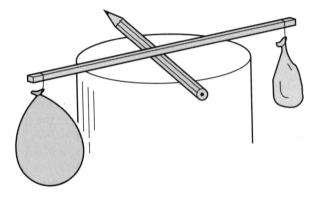

ideas. Within the groups there was considerable evidence of co-operation as well as tolerance of others' ideas.

One investigation to illustrate that 'air had weight' was to balance a stick, on a pencil, on top of a tin. The fulcrum point on the stick was marked with a pencil (Figure 4.2). Two balloons were attached to the ends of the sticks and the balance point checked. Then one balloon was blown up and reattached. The children predicted that the inflated balloon would 'go down' and their hypothesis for this was 'because air has weight'. When their predicted outcome occurred the children were confused and unhappy even though they had predicted correctly. One child said 'I've got the mark in the wrong place' and proceeded to change the pencil mark, indicating the point of balance, until the inflated balloon rose into the air. Another child said 'We've done it wrong' and even though he had written down his prediction he then finished his recording with an explanation as to what he thought should have happened.

These children had accepted the teacher's idea that air had weight, even though they had no evidence to support it and it contradicted their own ideas, that air was light or weightless. They were fully involved in the investigative procedure, but they had not planned the investigation out of their own explorations and observations and in answer to their own questions. During the activity they demonstrated good development of motivating attitudes, group participating attitudes and, to a lesser extent, investigating attitudes. The development of their reflective attitudes was very uncertain. They had firmly held ideas which contradicted the ideas of the teacher and, while they tolerated her ideas, they did not consider them in the final interpretation. They did not respect the evidence from their investigation when it challenged their ideas. It never occurred to them that the results could indicate that their ideas about 'light air', which led them to believe that the inflated balloon would rise, were incorrect. They were not flexible in their ideas and neither were they able to reflect critically on the investigation and see if the investigation was the cause for a discrepancy in their ideas and findings.

The classroom activity surrounding this work on air also illustrated an important factor affecting the development of children's attitudes *in* science and *to* science. During all the scientific explorations and investigations the children were obviously motivated, enthusiastic and curious. Some activities were very experiential and exploratory, while others, like the one described above, were more structured and had an expected outcome. I was very impressed with the children's involvement. At the end of a week of intense activity and development the children were asked to review their week and indicate what learning they had enjoyed and what learning they had disliked. Science did not fare very well during this evaluation. They had fun during the science activities but they did not like them. They did not like exploratory activities. They liked activities where a 'correct' answer resulted. They wanted assurances that they were progressing well, and science did not give them such assurances. Neither did they like activities which challenged their existing ideas. They wanted safety and confidence. They found this in a page of arithmetic which received a page of red ticks. This story illustrates the effect on scientific learning of the 'hidden curriculum' which is present in every school. Children, teachers and parents often have different views of education, different aims and different learning preferences and these can adversely affect the development of the child.

We all have different teaching and learning preferences (see Chapter 5). These preferences reflect the way all involved with the school view learning and form part of the learning milieu or school ethos, influencing both our attitudes to science as well as the choice of teaching and learning methods used by the teachers we encounter. The choice of teaching and learning method will actually form part of the total experience in science for learners and sends powerful messages about the nature of science.

Attitudes to science

We need to develop positive attitudes *to* science in children. The reasons why we need to do this can be considered from three different viewpoints: the viewpoint of the individual; the viewpoint of society; and the viewpoint of science and scientists.

Children as individuals need to have a positive image of science. By this I mean a full and accurate picture of the nature and different aspects of science. They need this positive image, not to coerce them into science as a career but to allow them to make an informed decision as to whether science has a part to play in their general lives. A full and accurate picture of science can assist children and adults in important decision-making, and without it understanding and interpretation of scientific issues within society are difficult (Millar and Wynne, 1988). These may be decisions which affect our immediate environment and the planet as a whole. For example, a full understanding of how science influences the environment allows us to make personal, local and national decisions, such as why we should recycle resources, why the local community needs a bypass and what the national government's policy on the disposal of hazardous waste should involve. An understanding of genetics and medical science allows us to make informed decisions as to the ethics and desirability of genetic engineering. Without the knowledge we are not in a position to make these decisions. This knowledge directly influences the attitudes we have about science. If our attitudes are based on accurate knowledge they are more likely to be positive than if based on hearsay and innuendo.

Positive attitudes to science are also important to society. Our society is 'dependent upon technology-based industrial and commercial activities' (Chemical Industries Association, 1994), and this has emphasized the need for greater scientific understanding to further good scientific and technological development. Greater scientific understanding will enable society to understand the effect of science, technology and industry on our environment and empower us as a society to make ecological decisions. There is also a need for good science graduates, equipped with relevant knowledge and skills, to further scientific and technological advances. There is concern that few young people who study science at school continue to study science at a higher level (Association for Science Education (ASE), 1994) or follow science career pathways (Millar and Wynne, 1988). Enthusiasm for science appears to be dwindling, and this may be due in part to the perception that science and technology will not aid successful future careers, particularly with respect to financial status. It may be a self-perpetuating cycle. Successful heads of industry are not scientists and therefore science is not the vehicle for success in industry. It may be, as Chapman (1991) has indicated, that a postindustrial society with diminishing employment for future generations will not need the emphasis we place on science in the National Curriculum – that is, unless we focus on the political and economic issues surrounding science to enable us as individuals and society to make important decisions with a global, national and individual perspective.

From the viewpoint of science and scientists, it is important to develop positive attitudes to science, to dispel the misconception that science is only appropriate for scientists. The mythical scientists are that strange breed of 'men', intelligent, grey-haired, bespectacled, eccentric, with test tubes or leaky pens in their pockets and a bemused expression on their faces, who muck up the environment (Figure 4.3). We only need to look as far as young children's pictures of scientists (Chambers, 1983) to see evidence of this image and to realize that it is not surprising that they do not see themselves as scientists (see also Figure 2.4, page 33).

Providing good role models in school and illustrating the differing part science plays in society will help to change the stereotyped view of science and the scientist. I would like children to be aware of the multifaceted, creative and qualitative aspects of science and to see its value in the widest sense, not, as I stated earlier, to coerce them into science as a career but to make them aware of its true nature and to decide for themselves the part it has to play in their lives.

As individuals we need to ask ourselves the question 'What is science?' We also need to help children to begin to answer the same question. The ideas people have about science can be divided into five categories, reflected in the following questions:

- Can science be *qualitative* in nature, or is it always *quantitative*?
- Is science *impersonal* or *personal*?

Figure 4.3 A scientist?

- Is it necessary always to be *objective* in science, or is there room to be *subjective*?
- Can science teaching accommodate differing views, that is, is it *value-free* or *value-dependent*?
- Does science carry its own *moral* code, or is it *amoral*?

Young children will have their own answers to a similar set of questions which will help to build up a picture of their attitudes to science:

- Who is a scientist?
- What do scientists do?
- Do scientists care for people, animals, plants?
- Can science help us?

Attitudes to science are affected by a number of influences in our lives (Figure 4.4). Some have already been touched upon in this book, but all are worth some in-depth consideration.

Figure 4.4   Influences in attitudes to science

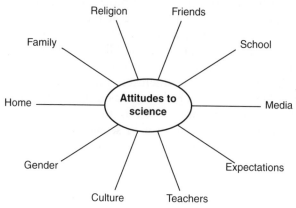

School and home

The school and the home are major influences on the development of children's attitudes to science. The attitudes towards science held outside school are likely to be mirrored in school and these can (Association for Science Education, 1993) include rather narrow views of science and scientists. The methods of teaching and learning in each area of knowledge send powerful messages about the knowledge itself. Is it difficult, boring, fun or interactive? Is it incomprehensible, logical or intuitive? Choices about teaching and learning methods are often made as a result of considerations such as organization, teachers' knowledge and background and the National Curriculum programmes of study. Children's expectations of science are the result of science experiences inside and outside school. They come to expect science to mean doing an investigation and drawing a picture or writing about it. Jarvis (1994) found that young children, when asked to draw pictures of scientists, often drew pictures of themselves or their teachers in school involved in a scientific activity. For these children science was something that happened in school. Some children also drew artists, and Jarvis (1994) felt that this was a result of the children being asked to draw a picture about their science activity. We do a science activity and then draw a picture. Therefore children believe science equals art.

During science activities interaction between the teacher and

the child occurs and through this a teacher will, often unconsciously, influence developing attitudes. The development of
attitudes to science can be influenced by the teacher's own preju-
dices, interests and ideas and can occur through unconscious
influences such as body language and linguistic emphases. Children will remember an enthusiastic teacher, and this enthusiasm
will influence the children's interest in the subject. Negative attitudes to science may adversely affect both the children's interest
and subsequent development. It is therefore important that
teachers have positive attitudes to science and science teaching in order to teach effectively and develop positive attitudes
in the children they teach. Teachers' attitudes to science have
developed in a similar way to those of the children they teach and
result from a complex of experiences gathered throughout their
lives, each with the potential to affect their attitudes in a different way. Very young children could be experiencing gravity
through dropping objects out of their pram. This may be a very
stimulating experience for them and end up being a game played
with adults. As they grow older they will have a variety of formal and informal science experiences which develop this initial
idea. They may make paper aeroplanes or explore the forces in
the water trough or bath. They may watch television programmes
or read textbooks about gravity and air resistance. Some of these
experiences may be positive and some negative and all provide
information about science. Together they provide an overall view
about science which will result in an attitude to science.

I have been aware of the effect of negative attitudes to science
from my own school experiences and from my earliest days of
primary teaching. My own background was one of varied science experiences. As a primary child I was part of the Nuffield
Primary Science Project (1964–6) and have memories of exciting science experiences. I can vividly remember, as an 11-year-
old, being very excited about the prospect of learning science in
the secondary school, but by the end of (what is now) Year 7 I
hated science. This affected my subsequent achievement in these
areas until, at a later date, I discovered the positive side of science through teaching. My own research (Hayes and Johnston,
1995; Johnston, 1995) is confirming the view (NCC, 1989; Harlen,
1992; Association for Science Education, 1993) that positive attitudes to science are important for scientific development and
can have an effect on the development of concepts and skills in

science. Primary initial teacher training needs to develop positive attitudes to science. I have become very concerned about the attitudes to science prevailing within the teaching community. As a primary school teacher I spent considerable time alleviating fears about science among my colleagues. More recently, at initial teacher training level, I have realized that many future teachers are fearful and concerned about science and teaching science in the primary classroom. Comments from primary initial teacher training students about the nature of science have included:

If it's science we are expected to . . . .
There's got to be a right answer.
I hate science, it's boring.
I can't do science, it's really hard.

These attitudes to science will be difficult to hide in the classroom and will inevitably have an effect on the children we teach. The effects of a limited view of science on the development of scientific skills and understanding were illustrated during an investigation with year 2 BEd students at Nottingham Trent University. When, working within the environment, students were asked to observe minibeasts and to carry out an investigation on the basis of their initial observations and explorations, one group decided to investigate which surfaces snails preferred. They designed an investigation which looked at the snails at regular intervals and noted where they were. After some time I asked them what they had discovered, and the reply was that the data collected had not been conclusive. I then asked them what surface they felt the snails preferred and they replied without hesitation 'the damp one . . . they went in there more often'. This example illustrated the students' views on the nature of science. It was about hard quantitative data, the only valid evidence being that collected at regular time intervals, with anything else being rejected as 'unscientific'.

Media

We have already mentioned the role of the media in developing ideas about science in Chapter 3. Children will recognize the mad scientist in media representations – the white-coated buffoon described earlier in this chapter. Figure 4.3 was drawn in response to my son's description of a scientist. As a Year 3 child he asked me 'Are you a real scientist, mummy?' He then went on to explain that he considered a 'real scientist' to 'have something to do with chemicals and things' (Johnston, 1992). He had been influenced by his limited experiences, which included television portrayals of scientists. When he saw the picture in Figure 4.3 he said 'That's a scientist'. I was dismayed by this narrow view of science and scientists even in such a young child and I was concerned with the number of children who acquire this view from the media and then have few other influences which challenge it. As children develop, the media view of science may, together with school experiences, confirm a view of science which is negative in nature (ASE, 1994).

Gender

From an early age girls can be discouraged from enjoying and achieving success in science by negative attitudes to science. Gender differences in attitudes have been found at all levels of development (Smail, 1984; Catsambis, 1995) although not in all studies (National Board of Employment, Education and Training, 1993). The development of attitudes to science is thought to occur early (Smail, 1984). Toys given to children send gender messages to them, and a child who uses construction toys and an electricity kit is likely to be confident and more able in science in the same way that one who plays with a doll is likely to be a more confident parent. Pre-school experience, together with role models, peer attitude, the media and a complex of other influences, means that girls often have a poor attitude and poor achievement in science subjects. Sometimes girls are discouraged by parents and teachers from taking science subjects. It is hardly surprising that this trend is reflected in the percentage of female undergraduates who study science-related subjects (Gold, 1990).

Culture

Cultural values can have a very large influence on the development of science in the primary school, especially where they conflict with the values traditionally viewed to be held by scientists. Science learning does not simply consist of acceptance of imparted ideas, especially when those ideas conflict with beliefs. Children may find ideas expressed within school controversial (Reiss, 1993) and they may even conflict with their beliefs, causing some alienation. Each science attainment target within the National Curriculum contains something which conflicts with the values held by some people within our society. Analysis of the National Curriculum not only identifies the conflicts, but together with consideration of the questions raised earlier in this chapter, can help individuals to decide on their view of the nature of science.

Attainment Target 1 (Experimental and Investigative Science) deals in part with the nature of science, which can be perceived in a variety of ways and will be affected by individual values. Is science about knowledge, facts and high intelligence? Is it creative and exploratory or repetitive and predictable? If children's views of the nature of science and scientists are limited, then it seems likely that their development as scientists will be affected.

Attainment Target 2 (Life Processes and Living Things) involves consideration of a number of ethical issues, even if political decisions appear to have removed them from the curriculum (DFE, 1995a). The subject of evolution (creation versus natural selection) can cause conflict, as can the area of reproduction and sex education and environmental issues such as recycling. I hope that the lack of emphasis on these issues is not a political and economic decision to remove them from the curriculum because schools' attempts to educate the whole person have addressed political and economic concerns (Chapman, 1991).

Attainment Target 3 (Materials and their Properties) involves work with materials and food technology and could expose conflicts regarding food beliefs. I once made the mistake of looking at the science involved in the baking process during Ramadan when a Muslim girl was fasting. Other food preferences need to be taken into consideration, as well as food allergies. Vegetarians would not welcome making bread with animal fat and sweets may put diabetics at risk.

The Earth and Beyond in Attainment Target 4 (Physical Processes) is not now specified as a requirement for Key Stage 1 children (DFE, 1995a) but poses additional problems concerned with scientific views of the birth of the universe, as compared to some religious teaching. Even as teachers of young children we cannot ignore these issues if they arise in the classroom, if for no other reason than that children will not stop asking profound questions about their origin even if the National Curriculum does not encourage it.

These areas of potential conflict make it necessary for all primary teachers to be aware of the need for sensitivity in teaching many aspects of science. Care needs to be taken to ensure that we do not indoctrinate children with our own cultural opinions, but provide a balanced view. The same areas of science can also provide opportunities to promote cultural similarities and celebrate differences, and this should also be remembered. For example, within Attainment Target 1 learning about scientists and the stories of science will help children to realize the differing views held by scientists and the differing lives of scientists. Children find the stories fascinating and are appalled to realize society's unjust treatment of some scientists. Antonouris (1991) and Reiss (1993) describe the life of Charles Drew, the black scientist who developed the blood bank and was then denied blood after a car crash. The stories of Marie Curie, Albert Einstein and many other famous scientists throughout the centuries can be retold easily to children of all ages, and make science and scientists more attainable and understandable for the average child. Children are more likely to remember the science if they can relate to the scientist. Learning about science is as important as learning science, and children need to have access to stories about scientific discoveries, theories and people. This will help them to realize that scientists are normal human beings, that science is relevant to their lives (Reiss, 1993), that science is not something that is only carried out by scientists in laboratories.

In Attainment Target 2 children can explore the similarities and differences between themselves. Shoe size, head size, height, food preferences and interests can be compared with beliefs and celebrations. There are some good activities which illustrate both similarities and differences. Focus on observable physical differences and similarities can lead to greater tolerance about differences, but care needs to be taken to ensure that differences are not ridiculed and that children are not made to feel inadequate. In Attainment Target 3 food preferences and food celebrations can develop cultural awareness, but again care needs to be taken to ensure that differences are treated sensitively and that beliefs are not ridiculed. A conflict of beliefs also exists within Attainment Target 4 (Physical Processes), where study of the Earth and Beyond may expose different cultural and religious ideas. However, sensitive handling can promote not only cultural awareness but also tolerance and acceptance.

Friends

It would be foolish to believe that children were not influenced by their peers. If friends have negative attitudes to science then this may influence children's attitudes, especially as they are forming. Peer-group pressures can influence children's development in the classroom in a number of ways. If the classroom atmosphere is not conducive to asking questions then children are less likely to raise questions. If the class considers science to be boring and useless or only for the boys, then children may not challenge this view because they would not wish to appear different from their peers. They may believe that this view is expected of them and conform in this way.

Family

Children's attitudes to science are formed as a result of influences before they arrive in school (Smail, 1984), earlier than 'most other subjects' (Harlen, 1985: 5), which indicates the profound influence of parents. ASE (1993) stresses the importance of parental attitudes and of providing information to parents and school governors so that they develop a greater understanding of the investigative process and science itself. Sometimes science can appear to alienate itself from the average parent because of scientific language. Sometimes scientists hold different notions about the world or assign different meanings to words. There are differences in the meaning of the word 'science' (Hayes and Johnston, 1995) as a result of differences in experiences. Science experiences which are limited to one area of science will consider science with this area to the fore. Environmental experiences may lead to an understanding of science which emphasizes the environment. Some school science experiences may lead to an understanding that science is only practical in nature or emphasize process skills above conceptual development. The language of science can send messages about science which will help to develop views of science. There are differences in the meanings of words such as 'force' and 'energy' which have a common usage as well as a scientific usage. Ideas about the meanings of words such as 'exploratory' and 'practical' may differ in meaning or scope. The most worrying perception that parents can hold is that science, while important, has no part to play in their lives. There appear to be many families who feel that science is not

applicable to their lives (Johnston, 1995), and there is a gap between the perceptions that parents have of science and the part
that science plays in individual lives. A parent who makes wine
at home may understand the wine-making process but believe
he/she understands little or no chemistry. A keen gardener can
be an amateur ecologist and have a good understanding of the
environment. A snooker player must be able to understand forces
and their effects. A dog breeder must have some understanding
of genetics. If we are removing stains from clothes we must be
able to identify which soap powders are the most effective and
understand something about materials and their properties.

Science plays an important part in all our lives. To provide a
coherent understanding of science we need to be aware of this
and of the full nature of science.

A multifaceted approach to developing positive attitudes to science

Developing attitudes to science needs to take into account the different influences on that development. I call this a multifaceted
approach to the development of attitudes (see Figure 4.5). It needs
to consider the development of attitudes in teachers, parents and
children. Teacher training, both initial training and in-service,
needs to focus on what positive attitudes to science are, whether
we have positive attitudes and how they can be developed in the
children we teach. School curricular developments should help
to improve children's attitudes through good teaching, creative
activities, sensitivity to the values and opinions of others, school
visits and special events such as science and technology weeks
and inter-school egg races. The development of positive parental
attitudes can involve greater participation in school science. They
can include home–school science liaison and special school events
to focus on science in the curriculum or the nature of science,
such as science fairs and industry links (Woolnough, 1994).

My concern about the influence of negative or limited parental attitudes to science on children in school led, in 1993, to the
development of an experiential workshop to develop positive
attitudes to and a better understanding of science in primary
school parents and governors. This workshop (Eland *et al.*, 1995a;
1995b; 1995c; 1995d; 1995e) is supported by Nottingham Trent

Figure 4.5 How can we encourage positive attitudes to science?

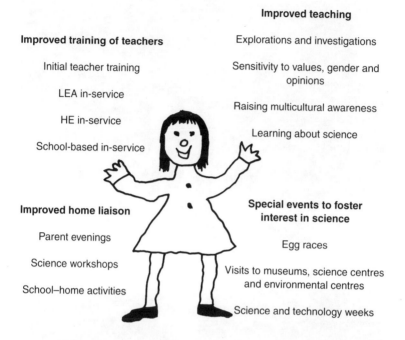

Improved teaching

Improved training of teachers

Initial teacher training

LEA in-service

HE in-service

School-based in-service

Explorations and investigations

Sensitivity to values, gender and opinions

Raising multicultural awareness

Learning about science

Improved home liaison

Parent evenings

Science workshops

School–home activities

Special events to foster interest in science

Egg races

Visits to museums, science centres and environmental centres

Science and technology weeks

University and the Royal Society's Committee on the Public Understanding of Science. It was felt to be of great importance in supporting schools in their efforts to develop positive attitudes in children through the activities undertaken as part of the National Curriculum. Through the workshop parents, governors, teachers and children are able to work together to develop a greater understanding of the nature of science to the mutual benefit of individuals, education and science. Our workshop initiative was an extension of this work undertaken in individual schools and was an attempt to make the effects of such work more widespread and support a larger number of schools.

The activities within the workshop were designed as examples of good primary science practice, in that they identified the dual nature of science process and knowledge. All activities involve experiencing science knowledge through initial curiosity and active participation, in the belief that 'positive attitudes can be developed through activities which are themselves interesting and thought-provoking, and which can harness . . . natural curiosity

Parents, teachers and children exploring science together

and questioning' (Raper and Stringer, 1987: 20). There are 30 self-contained activities on light, electricity, energy, forces and materials. Each activity follows a questioning approach which is designed to encourage participants to explore the concept, focus on specific aspects, and undertake simple investigations. There are then suggestions for simple investigations which could be followed up in the home. Throughout the workshop the aim is to challenge (often deep-rooted) perceptions of science. The workshop has been developed to provide flexibility in delivery, hopefully making it more appropriate to individual schools' needs and abilities, and is available for use in schools. The interactions of parents involved in the workshop have been interesting. Many never get past the period of free exploration but for them the process of exploration has been extremely useful and probably sufficient. Quite a number of people have interacted with the questions and focused their exploration, although some of these do not interact in the expected way. For example, one group of parents was observed responding to the question, 'How can you make light shine round a corner?', by using mirrors which had been joined together to put into a kaleidoscope. It appeared that they felt that the problem must involve some complex scientific equipment. Another parent observing this interaction commented 'Did you ever do that at school? Use a mirror to shine a light in someone's face?' The response was 'Oh yes, but I didn't think that was science.'

Home–school liaison is not exceptional. There is good practice throughout England in individual schools and local groups as well as national projects linking home and school such as *School Home Investigations in Primary Science* (Solomon and Lee, 1991). There are even international initiatives such as the proposal to establish the European Research Network About Parents in Education (ERNAPE) which aims to disseminate information regarding current research in this field and assist in developing contacts. Success in developing positive attitudes in science and to science depends on all parties concerned in the process – parents, teachers, children and society. We all need to play our part.

Summary

- Positive attitudes are necessary in science and to science.
- Attitudes in science can be categorized into motivating attitudes,

group participating attitudes, investigating attitudes and reflective attitudes.
- Attitudes to science are the result of a complex of influences on children's lives. Work to develop attitudes to science should adopt a multifaceted approach which addresses these influences.

Useful reading

Clarke, B. (1989) *Women and Science*. Hove: Wayland.

Conner, E. (1987) *Great Lives. Marie Curie*. Hove: Wayland.

Craig, J. (1988) Girl-friendly or boy-friendly teaching styles. *Primary Science Review*, 6: 25–6.

Hobden, J. (1993) Do children see themselves as real scientists? *Primary Science Review*, 28: 6–7.

Kingsley, N. (1989) *Benjamin Franklin*. Hatfield: Association for Science Education.

Kingsley, N. (1989) *Louis Pasteur*. Hatfield: Association for Science Education.

Morgan, N. (1993) *Famous Scientists*. Hove: Wayland.

Pateman, T. (1990) Dinosaurs are not enough! *Primary Science Review*, 13: 29.

Solomon, J. (1989) *The Search for Simple Substances*. Hatfield: Association for Science Education.

Solomon, J. (1989) *Discovering the Cure for Scurvy*. Hatfield: Association for Science Education.

5

Developing the teacher's role

The role of the teacher is an essential part of the learning process. The teaching role in primary science will reflect the teacher's philosophy on teaching in general, and teaching primary science in particular. A teaching philosophy develops as a result of scientific understanding, personal experiences and reflection on those understandings and experiences. School and home science experiences, initial teacher training and teaching experiences will all be of influence here. Teachers enter the teaching profession with their own personal beliefs about education which include ideas on the professionalism of the teacher, the teacher's role, the value and nature of primary science education, the aim of primary science education and what good primary science teaching involves. Sometimes these beliefs are limited in breadth and depth (Hayes and Johnston, 1995) but they are likely to reflect the beliefs within the wider society.

We only need to listen to news broadcasts or read the newspapers to realize that it is not just teachers entering the profession who have quite firm philosophies on education; we all have.

Hardly a week goes by without someone saying what schools should do or what their responsibilities are. All of society has an opinion on the purpose of primary education, what primary education should include and how schools should achieve the numerous demands made upon them. It is understandable that all of society should have an opinion about education. Individuals within society have all experienced education, and this experience has enabled them to formulate firm ideas about it. Unfortunately these experiences also lead individuals to believe they are knowledgeable about all aspects of education even if their experiences have been limited and their knowledge does not give them a broad overview of education.

Cultural differences in philosophies of science education will also be reflected within the teaching profession (Hayes and Johnston, 1995) and the wider society. The cultural emphases of the Finnish and English educational systems with regard to science were considered in Chapter 1, with the Finnish educational system reflecting an environmental emphasis and the English system a scientific process emphasis. Both educational systems are undergoing significant changes in terms of teaching approaches (Hayes and Johnston, 1993), and this reflects historical cultural and philosophical emphases. In England and Wales, our approaches before 1991 had developed out of an established philosophy of teaching, historical research and observation of practice. Finland is at a crossroads created from the opposite perspective. There has been a Finnish National Curriculum for some time and Finland is now seeking a new approach to interest and motivate children.

Within the school, individual philosophies are shared and mixed, and the result is a school philosophy which, like the new level descriptions for assessment, is a best-fit scenario. Individual teachers within the school need to debate their beliefs and come to a common understanding or a common belief about their educational aims and objectives and how they can best be achieved. Working together inevitably means that some individual ideas will not fit the school philosophy, but it is essential that teachers work towards a common aim and have a common understanding of how that aim can best be achieved. This may mean that individuals need to modify their philosophies, or shelve aspects of them until changes in school, staff or educational climate make them more generally acceptable. Major differences in beliefs and practices can lead to discontinuity for children. The most advantageous aspect of the National Curriculum is that for the first time in national education in England and Wales, all children should receive similar science experiences during compulsory schooling, particularly at Key Stages 1 to 3. However, the experiences of learning may be quite different and, while it is important that children develop the ability to learn in a variety of situations, it is important also that children who have these experiences do not have their development impaired or slowed by discontinuity. I am not suggesting that all primary teachers should teach science in the same way, but I am indicating that schools need to plan not only for the science content, but also for the method of delivery. In my early years of teaching, little debate about the teacher's role, curriculum organization and learning preferences occurred, and I am aware that my own teaching did little to provide continuity for the children. Within a school, children could move from teacher-directed learning to more flexible learning situations and then to didactic teaching situations, and there was no consideration of how they would benefit from these teaching and learning situations, what messages about science were being given or how effective their scientific development was.

Most school science policies reflect the need to meet the aims of the National Curriculum and contain statements to that effect, but they also indicate how science should be taught within the school and the underlying philosophy of the school. They indicate whether science should

- be part of topic work within the school;
- be a distinctly separate part of the curriculum;
- be planned rigidly throughout the school;
- meet certain objectives at different stages;
- stem from the children's explorations;
- be guided by the teacher.

Continuity within a school implies consistency in aims, values and expectations. Teachers within a school should have a shared philosophy of education and be working towards a common educational goal. Continuity does not imply uniformity of experience. Teachers' individual creativity and style should not be affected by continuity. It also implies good teacher relationships within the school. A school can achieve continuity through a team-work approach to policy, planning and teaching. This could involve joint policy decisions and sharing of philosophy, goals and modes of delivery. It could involve shared planning for one year, one key stage, or throughout primary schooling. It could involve the sharing of ideas for activities and effective teaching styles, it could involve teaching to strengths and expertise throughout a year or the whole school or it could include shared teaching. My own teaching experience has been diverse. I have taught in situations where there was little continuity and few agreed aims, but also in others where team work was highly valued in order to meet the schools' aims. In one school I was responsible for the planning and teaching of the whole science curriculum; in another year groups planned together and team teaching ensured best use of curriculum expertise and provided an element of staff development. Whatever the school's way of working, full commitment was essential in order to achieve continuity in science teaching and learning. Teachers needed to agree on a school philosophy on science education and find out both the children's and their colleagues' working preferences and plan to accommodate these and the goals set by the National Curriculum in science. Discussion and planning are the keys to effective scientific development and teachers need to plan

- for the teacher's role;
- for the children's learning;
- for the context of learning;
- for the organization of effective learning.

Planning for the teacher's role

Decisions about the role of the teachers are important in the development of a motivating learning environment. There have been a number of attempts to categorize the role of the teacher (Richards, 1984; Rowland, 1984; Osborne and Freyberg, 1985; Harlen, 1992; Fleer, 1993) and the resulting teaching and learning styles. Most of us, like Harlen (1992), advocate a child-centred approach to teaching and learning but, hopefully, we would not use one teaching approach exclusively (School Curriculum and Assessment Authority (SCAA), 1994c) and would, as Alexander *et al.* (1992) hope, review the balance between direct and indirect teaching approaches. With each approach the teacher's role will differ, but I believe that the main feature of the teacher's role remains the same, that is, that the teacher is a facilitator of learning rather than an imparter of knowledge. This role hinges on the belief that teaching and learning are not passive experiences in which the teacher imparts knowledge to the learner, who is then able to use or apply that learning in everyday life. Teaching and learning are active experiences involving significant interactions between the teacher and the learner and others who influence development (see Figure 4.4). This idea is not new and is embodied in many of the already identified teaching and learning approaches. This view of the teacher also embodies the teaching roles identified by Osborne and Freyberg (1985), of motivator, diagnostician, guide, innovator, experimenter and researcher. Consideration of some teaching and learning approaches in primary science can help us to identify these teaching roles. In looking at these approaches we should remember that teachers use a variety of approaches in their teaching (SCAA, 1994c), and that different approaches have different uses and advantages.

An instructional approach

This approach involves the teacher as an imparter of knowledge, and while it cannot alone develop skills and conceptual understanding, it does have a place in the early years classroom. During a scientific exploration children will need some teacher guidance, direction or even instruction to enable them to succeed. While exploring fabrics, Darren and Paul decided to find out which material was the warmest. The idea for exploration was decided by the teacher but they decided what focus their investigation would take. They needed help in the planning of an investigation to ensure that it would be successful. This help took the form of listening to their ideas and guiding them towards consideration of the variables involved. An initial idea was to make a glove out of each material and see which glove was the warmest. The teacher helped them to make a mitten with each piece of material which they put on their hands in the cold playground. They made qualitative judgements about the warmth of the materials, but some were difficult to separate and there was disagreement between the boys. The teacher suggested that they measured how warm the mittens kept something by using a thermometer. They then decided to put something hot into each mitten and take the temperature. The teacher suggested they cover a plastic cup containing warm water with each mitten. Before they could do this the children needed some instruction on how to use a thermometer, and guidance on how and when to take the temperatures.

This investigation was initiated by the children, guided by the teacher and then needed some specific teaching to ensure its successful outcome. The teacher's role changed throughout the activity from motivator and guide (Osborne and Freyberg, 1985) to instructor (Rowland, 1984). Some instruction or prompting is necessary in every exploration and investigation with young children. Sometimes it is to ensure the success of the activity, sometimes to show the use of scientific equipment, and sometimes it is to ensure the safe handling of living things. Simon *et al.* (1992a; 1992b) defined 'openness' in science in terms of three continua – defining the problem, choosing the methods, and arriving at solutions – and the amount of openness can differ in each one. In this way, the teacher provides more support when needed but can also allow children to make their own decisions about their learning.

We also use more instructional teaching methods in 'carpet time' with young children. Teachers of Key Stage 1 children often use carpet time at the beginning and end of teaching sessions. This time is of great use in setting tasks, motivating the children, organizing the activities, discussing ideas and interpreting from activities. It is also a time when the role of the teacher becomes more instructional. The children may need instructions as to how to behave in the classroom, how to use resources and what the expected outcome is. It may be, as described in Chapter 2, that one group of children become guides and instructors for the other children by describing their explorations and ideas and helping other children to build upon their work. The hard task for a teacher is knowing when to be instructional and when not to be. In observations of adults interacting with children, I have noticed some interesting trends regarding the teaching role. Inexperienced student teachers and parents tend to take on the instructional role to a greater extent and 'teach' the children. They appear constrained by their lack of confidence in science and their limited understanding of the nature of science. There is a body of scientific knowledge which needs to be imparted to the child. The teacher/adult is expected to have access to this body of knowledge and can be an 'authoritative instructor' (Rowland, 1981). More experienced teachers, and student teachers with greater scientific understanding and confidence in the classroom, tend to be less didactic and instructional and take on the role of the teacher as motivator and guide. This occurs as their confidence and experience grow.

A discovery approach

Inherent in the discovery approach to learning in science is the desire to provide a motivating environment in which children learn through exploration. The narrow view of discovery science is that children take on the role of scientists and make new discoveries for themselves. The danger here is that they may not discover anything or that they are looking to see what the hidden agenda of the teacher is. Discovery science has a special place in the Key Stage 1 classroom. Discovery is very appropriate for early years children because there is so much more to discover when you are five years of age than when you are 10 or 13 years of age, but it should be used with caution to ensure that the children are making good use of their learning time.

Harlen (1992) identifies the dangers of using a discovery approach in isolation and uses Driver *et al.*'s (1985) argument that older children are quick to see that there is always a purpose to their discovery – something they are expected to find out. I do not believe that discovery learning has to mean that the children discover what it is they have to learn before they can actually learn it. We should always be clear about the purposes of our activities, our learning objectives, and if we share these with the children they can have more ownership of their learning and they have a better chance of being successful. However, if we embark on a discovery approach to learning with specific learning purposes we may be unsuccessful. A discovery approach is often more successful if used with no specific learning aims and objectives in mind. This means that, like the ice balloon activity described in Chapters 1 and 2, it could develop knowledge within a number of scientific concepts, as well as a number of differing skills or attitudes. No one particular aim will have been identified in advance by the teacher. Rather, it is the learner who identifies which area of interest to pursue and the teacher responds to this. On the other hand, discovery learning stemming from an ice balloon exploration could aim to develop particular skills, knowledge or attitudes and therefore have a specific learning focus. For example, it could aim to develop knowledge about the properties of water or the skill of observation or curiosity. It could develop knowledge about floating and sinking or planning an investigation or skills involved with group planning and co-operation. I often use such an approach in early years teaching and in introducing primary science to adults. Discovering ice balloons is a good example as the resulting development in skills and concepts can be varied.

Another discovery activity I have used stems from the 'discovery box'. I have a collection of boxes, plastic tubs and tins of different shapes and sizes and each one contains different objects. One may contain a collection of different springs, another some feathers, another some leaves and another some magnets and some paper clips. I use these boxes in a number of ways. We can play a guessing game to see if the children can guess what is in the box. They may use contextual clues such as the shape or size of the box or what it was produced for (eggs, margarine, chocolates). They may use their senses and weigh or feel the box or shake it and listen to the sound inside. Once they have opened the box and removed the contents they can explore them and ask questions about them. The avenues for discovery are varied and although each box will probably have limited scope I have been surprised by the diversity of explorations. To take the assortment of feathers, children can explore their structure, using magnifiers to look closely at them or projecting them or part of them on to a screen. They can also look at how they fall through the air, comparing them with how other objects fall. I have seen children look at the patterns on feathers or see how good different feathers are for painting or writing.

The role of the teacher in such a discovery approach is changeable. The teacher is a motivator and innovator (Osborne and Freyberg, 1985) in providing resources and a motivating force to encourage learning. He/she is also responsible for guiding the children's learning to ensure that they are able to explore effectively, raise questions which can be explored further and make sense of their discoveries. In some cases the discovery approach can be used with a learning focus in mind. It may be that you wish to guide the children's discoveries on ice balloons to look at melting and solidifying. You may plan the contents of the 'discovery boxes' to focus on a particular concept, such as forces. The contents of the boxes would reflect the concept. Within the concept of forces, feathers, springs, plasticine balls and different grades of sandpaper can all be used as contents of the boxes. This is a more guided discovery approach and again is very appropriate for young learners.

A problem-solving approach

Problem-solving provides a good link with science and technology in the classroom. It can also provide a motivating context for children's learning. The problem of which glove is the warmest (see above) is especially motivating when it is a problem initiated by the children from their own explorations. Problems can also be set by the teacher, but care needs to be taken to ensure that such problems are motivating for the children and appear to have a real purpose.

While problem-solving can be a motivating link between primary science and technology, it can also create a dilemma about the form and purpose of science and technology in the primary classroom. Primary science can be described as developing scientific concepts, skills and attitudes through practical activities, whereas primary technology, in part, can be described as the application of some scientific concepts and skills through practical activity such as problem-solving. The dilemma occurs because in the primary classroom children are often undertaking both activities simultaneously and because, in such a situation, scientific development may be limited. Children may be set a problem to solve such as which type of paper will make the strongest tower. They may successfully plan a problem-solving investigation to make towers using different papers and test them fairly. They could be following the scientific process, and from their investigation they could solve the problem and decide which paper made the strongest tower, but there may have been little development of their scientific concepts and knowledge. Such an activity will 'involve the application of scientific ideas but perhaps not the development of these ideas if the activity stops at the point of solving the problem' (Harlen, 1992: 47).

A good problem-solving activity would start from the children's interests. The teacher's role would be to guide the children, defining an initial problem or initiating the problem with guidance from the children. Some guidance or instruction would be needed to enable the problem-solving to continue. However, if the problem-solving pathways had already been defined, the role would be more instructional. The problem with predefining the problem-solving pathway is that ownership and motivation may be lost and possible learning limited. A more guided role would allow for greater motivation and subsequent learning. A third role which could be adopted within a problem-solving approach is that of flexible interactor, where the teacher interacts with the children, asking questions which will focus on the scientific learning in the activity, ensuring that the children's scientific development is forwarded.

A focused approach

This approach to learning can take a number of forms. A focused investigation would have a specific scientific aim or focus. This may be initiated by the teacher or by the teacher in conjunction with the children. The teacher may decide that this term's work in science should focus on the human body. Activities are planned with this focus in mind, taking into consideration any previous school work on the human body and the requirements of the National Curriculum. A focused approach can also arise out of exploration, with children observing phenomena and raising questions for further exploration and investigation. These questions can then be sorted by the teacher who decides a focus for the work, or by the teacher and children who jointly decide the focus for exploration and investigation. This approach (see Table 5.1) contains elements of Harlen's (1992) and Faire and Cosgrove's (1988) 'interactive teaching' model, Osborne and Freyberg's (1985) 'generative learning' model, and the 'constructivist learning' model of the Children's Learning in Science Project (CLISP) 1982–9 (Scott, 1987) and the SPACE Project CRIPSAT, 1986–90 (Osborne *et al.*, 1992). The focus can emerge or be modified from the children's interests and questions raised, ideas and previous knowledge or from interaction between interests and ideas. The teaching role is as a motivator and interactor, encouraging and motivating

Table 5.1 Models of teaching and learning

Interactive teaching (Harlen, 1992; Faire and Cosgrove, 1988)	Generative learning (Osborne and Freyberg, 1985)	Constructivist learning (Scott, 1987)
• Preparation • 'Before' views of children • Exploratory activities • Children's questions • Investigations • 'After' views of children • Reflection	• Preliminary phase • Focus phase • Challenge phase • Application	• Orientation • Elicitation of ideas • Restructuring of ideas • Application of ideas • Review change in ideas

the children and interacting with their ideas and interests, to forward their scientific development.

An exploratory approach

An exploratory approach can be looked upon as a form of discovery learning in which the teacher and child negotiate an experience for the child, which is later evaluated by both the teacher and the child (Rowland, 1984). I prefer to consider this as an approach which utilizes the best aspects of all approaches in an attempt not to 'throw out the baby with the bathwater'. An exploratory approach may contain aspects from all the approaches described above and be very appropriate for the younger learner.

The teaching role is varied throughout the learning activity. It may begin with some 'carpet time' where the teacher as a motivator stimulates the children and encourages their explorations. The children will then have opportunities to explore a range of phenomena with the teacher acting as a guide, helping the children to observe and raise questions which can be further explored or investigated. The teacher may then act as a convener, assembling the children and making sense of their ideas for further exploration and investigation. The teacher may decide to group children together on the basis of their ideas or needs, or focus the children's ideas to enable them to undertake a specific learning pathway. It may mean that the teacher needs to take on the role of instructor, in giving the children specific instructions on how to use a piece of equipment, or how their exploration or investigation would best proceed. During the next stage of exploration and investigation, the teacher would continue as a motivator, but would also take on the role of interactor, asking questions to extend the children's thinking or encourage the development of their skills. Finally, the teacher would draw together the emerging ideas and hypotheses resulting from the activity and take on the role of convener in order to disseminate ideas and challenge misconceptions.

In an effective exploratory approach to teaching and learning science the teacher would plan for his/her part in the teaching and learning process. The teacher would share his/her philosophy of education with colleagues, decide on a school philosophy and aims, plan for continuity of teaching and learning within the school and plan his/her role in the teaching and learning process.

Planning for children's learning

Learning implies there is a gap between children's existing ideas and the ideas that we aim for them to develop. One of the teacher's roles is to gain access to the children's existing ideas and to make professional decisions as to how they can be developed, modified or changed and the gap closed. For some children this gap exists because of poor preparation for school (Donaldson, 1978). This is why a multifaceted approach to development, as described in Chapter 4, is so important. If we wish to close the learning gap, we need to engage in a partnership with children and parents as well as teaching colleagues, to plan a teaching and learning pathway which will best meet our educational aims and objectives, the children's needs and abilities and the requirements of the National Curriculum.

Primary science before the introduction of the National Curriculum debated the merits of process skill development or concept development. Assessment within the National Curriculum appears to put the emphasis on conceptual development, but I prefer to believe that a combination of conceptual, skill and attitude development is preferable and that the National Curriculum's apparent lack of emphasis on all three equally is due to the difficulties of assessing skills and attitudes, not because they are unimportant. Planning for teaching and learning in primary science needs to take into consideration needs and abilities in terms of concepts, knowledge, skills and attitudes. These needs and abilities can be ascertained in a number of ways.

Planning for the development of scientific skills

Children can be observed while they are exploring and their skills can be noted. Asking questions can help to focus on their skills. For example, if we ask children to tell us about the differences between different objects during a floating and sinking exploration, we can ascertain their observational skills. If they are able to raise questions from their observations, such as 'Do all wooden objects float?' or 'Why do some things seem to float and sink?', we can ascertain their skills in raising questions. Listening to their discussions can tell us if they are able to hypothesize about why some objects float or sink: 'I think all these things will float because they are little.' We can observe children planning investigations and ascertain their ability to plan, make predictions, measure and record data, and we can question them about their investigations or analyse their written work, drawings or any other records. We can also see how they have drawn together their ideas and begun to interpret their data (Cavendish *et al.*, 1990).

Planning for the development of scientific skills involves the teacher in identifying the needs and abilities of the children, deciding how these skills develop, providing opportunities for the development to occur and facilitating that development. In deciding to develop observational skills with young children, teachers should provide exploratory opportunities for close observation to occur. Children should be encouraged to use their full senses in their observations. The provision of observational aids should assist observation. The children should then be encouraged to notice small details in their observations as well as similarities and differences between things. It may also be appropriate to make sense of observations through classification. The skills of science cannot effectively be developed in isolation and there needs to be meaningful scientific content developed

Figure 5.1 Finding out about children

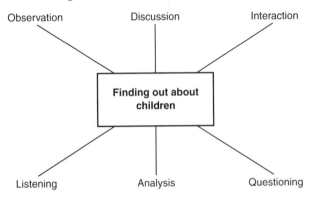

alongside skills (McClelland, 1983). The relationship between skills and concepts, described in Chapter 2 as spiralling together like a double helix, should be remembered when planning for teaching and learning.

Planning for conceptual development

The importance of eliciting children's existing ideas is widely accepted (see Scott, 1987 for the Children's Learning in Science (CLIS) project; Harlen, 1992; see Osborne 1992 for the Centre for Research in Primary Science and Technology (CRIPSAT) SPACE project), and becomes more important when we become aware of children's varied ideas and the differing ways these ideas develop. The work of Piaget (1929) did much to advance our knowledge of how children's ideas develop. More recent work by the CLIS 1982–9 and SPACE 1986–90 projects has highlighted some of the common scientific misconceptions that children hold and the way some conceptual development occurs. The implications of the research findings are clear. Effective teaching and learning are dependent on children's existing ideas and rely on knowledge of these ideas and subsequent good teaching. We need to ascertain the ideas children hold and the influences on their ideas before we can plan to develop their ideas further, modify their ideas or change them completely. Learning is not simply a matter of adding to and extending existing concepts. It may necessitate radical reorganization of existing thinking. We should also remember that children, like those described in Chapter 4, may resist new ideas, hold contradictory ideas or even change their ideas depending on the context. In familiar contexts children may develop new or more sophisticated ideas but revert to more simplistic ideas in an unfamiliar context. If we are to develop, modify or change children's ideas we need time to find out those ideas and to plan appropriate activities to challenge them. We also need additional time for reflection to consolidate new or more developed ideas. This is the basis of constructivist learning as outlined by the Children's Learning in Science (CLIS) 1982–9 (Scott, 1987) project; the remodification of any misconceptions and new learning occurs when individual children are allowed to construct their own meaning through experience with the physical environment and through social interaction. This is an active and continuous process whereby children construct links with their prior knowledge, generating new ideas, checking and restructuring old ideas or hypotheses.

In this way learning in science is not passive and children are responsible for controlling their own learning. The first phase of constructivist learning is the orientation phase, where the concept is examined and children's ideas are elicited. The techniques in Figure 5.1 can also be used to find out children's ideas in a particular concept area. Analysis of children's work can include writing, stories and pictures. In each case, discussion about the work is essential to ensure that you understand the child's view of the world. Another useful way to ascertain children's conceptual ideas is to analyse concept maps (Novak and Gowan, 1984). Concept maps look similar to 'brainstorming' spiders' webs used to map out ideas for planning. However, they are more organized than these spiders' webs, in that they indicate perceived relationships between concepts. Children can use an already prepared list of words related to a concept or brainstorm their own. These words are then linked using appropriate words.

Andrew's first attempt at a concept map (Figure 5.2) is very simple but shows his thinking on the theme of ice. It is important to find time to discuss with children the ideas they have expressed in their maps. Analysis of Andrew's map indicated that he saw the process of melting and solidifying as a one-way process, and it was important to clarify this before planning and further development could continue. The discussion with Andrew

Figure 5.2   Andrew's concept map

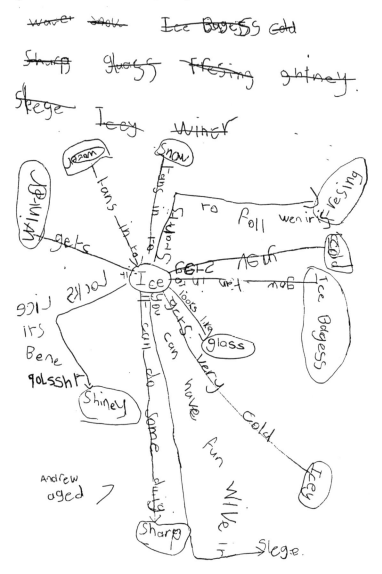

about his concept map was essential to elicit his ideas. The map alone can only give an indication of his thinking. Concept mapping has been found to be a useful tool by teachers to ascertain children's existing ideas, begin the process of introducing a theme and inform planning. Teachers have also used concept mapping to give children more independence in assessing their own knowledge and limitations and to begin to identify their own learning needs. It is important to remember that it is not a tool that will necessarily be successful when first used, as children may need some experience in this way of mapping out their ideas. It would also not be useful to use it on too regular a basis as children may find it tedious. Cross (1992) used pictorial concept maps with young children who found writing difficult. Group concept maps can also be useful, but in order to inform planning to match children's needs and abilities it is most important to listen to the interactions during the mapping and to question children about their emerging ideas.

The next phase in constructivist learning involves the restructuring of ideas. For this to occur the teacher needs clarification of the ideas elicited using a variety of techniques, such as illustrated in Figure 5.1. Once this has occurred the teacher's role involves planning for experiences which will develop, modify or change existing ideas. This may involve the children in situations where their ideas are challenged and refuted, and this may cause some frustration. It is important that each child experiences some success and that any feelings of frustration are harnessed to motivate and not demotivate. During planned activities the teacher should gauge the learning situation and be flexible enough to change plans in order to achieve development. The teacher also needs to interact with the children and guide their activity so that new ideas can be constructed by them and they have opportunities to reflect on their old ideas and emerging new ideas. New or modified ideas are fragile and need nurturing. The children need time to consider them and opportunities to apply them in other situations. This will not only help to clarify ideas but to develop them further. As children's ideas are developed and reviewed they will be able to use them in a variety of situations both familiar and unfamiliar. They should also be able to link complex and abstract phenomena together. Revisiting their original concept maps at this stage can be useful to consolidate new ideas developed through teaching.

Table 5.2   Ways of learning in science and about science

Listening to other children	Watching science television programmes
Listening to teachers	Following worksheet activities
Using the computer	Discussing ideas with children and
Investigating your own	teachers
ideas	Planning individual projects
Reading books	Copying from a book, worksheet or the
Visits to museums, science	board
centres	Planning work with others in a group

Planning for the development of attitudes

Chapter 4 identified the need to develop children's attitudes in science and attitudes to science. The techniques in Figure 5.1 also apply here. Listening to children engaged in their work will help to identify their attitudes in and to science, as will questioning them and discussing their ideas. Drawing pictures of scientists can also be revealing (Chambers, 1983) but it is essential that children have an opportunity to explain their ideas and pictures. This will enable us to look at science from the children's perspective and prevent us from making assumptions about their attitudes based on our own experiences and views.

Learning preferences are likely to affect and be affected by attitudes in and to science. Planning should take children's learning preferences into consideration. There are many ways in which we can learn and these are listed in Table 5.2. We all have preferred ways of learning. Many children and adults would prefer passive learning and it would be wonderful if knowledge, skills and attitudes could be imparted to us with little or no personal effort. But passive learning is not a reality. We need to be part of the learning process, whatever learning method is used and whatever our learning preference. If we read a book or watch a television programme, learning will not occur unless we participate in some way, and willing, active participation will achieve greater development. We are not always aware that we are participating but it is necessary for learning of any kind to take place. Some learning preferences do appear to need less participation but I would argue that unless we are fully engaged in the concepts, knowledge and skills involved then learning will not be fully effective and may even be impaired. More passive forms of learning are also less likely to develop scientific skills and this is an additional reason in support of active learning. In planning for scientific development we need to plan to widen learning preferences, to enable children to learn in a variety of situations and through a variety of media. For Key Stage 1 children, practical experience is essential and cannot be replaced. Secondary sources such as books, television and worksheets can be used to initiate or back up practical learning but cannot replace it. Again we need a multifaceted approach to learning.

Planning for the learning context

The context of learning is another essential ingredient of an effective early years classroom.

Children require an atmosphere which will nurture learning, allow ideas to be freely expressed and enable failure to develop into success, without any associated fears. As with all aspects of learning, home–school partnership is important. If children find school an alien environment they are less likely to learn. The more prepared children are for school life and the more prepared the teacher is for the child's development the more successful learning will be. Harlen (1977b: 4–5) describes an atmosphere conducive to learning as

a helping atmosphere; an atmosphere which encourages in each child enthusiasm for and concern about his work; which avoids boredom and frustration, which gives each child security and offers him the freedom of choice which is appropriate to his level of development and past experience.

An atmosphere in which children are able to express themselves without their ideas being belittled and where they can be motivated to develop new ideas or expand their ideas would constitute a 'helping atmosphere'. The classroom atmosphere is dependent upon relationships within the school and between school and home. In the classroom the children need to respect the needs of others and the class rules. This respect should help to establish the classroom atmosphere. Children need to have a relationship with the teacher built on trust where they feel able to express their ideas and concerns, and this should extend to other children in the class. Within the school, a helping atmosphere can be developed through shared aims, rules and educational philosophy.

Scientific development will also be assisted if the learning context starts from the familiar and progresses to the unfamiliar. Both teacher and child feel more confident with familiar phenomena and once both feel secure and are motivated unfamiliar phenomena seem less threatening. Another advantage of using familiar objects and events in science is that it will help to establish the everyday nature of science. Science will then cease to be something which only occurs in the laboratory or classroom and will become something which is observable in all aspects of life. Exploring a range of everyday materials or bubbles using different washing-up liquids is less threatening than using prisms, lenses and electrical equipment, although we should not underestimate the motivating force of 'scientific' resources in some situations. Scientific development will also be assisted if the context is cross-curricular and not focused on specific scientific concepts. There have been many advocates of cross-curricular teaching or thematic teaching (Department of Education and Science, 1985; Association for Science Education *et al.*, 1989; Harlen and Jelly, 1989). Critics (Alexander *et al.*, 1992) appear to be advocating greater emphasis on effective teaching methods, rather than criticizing thematic teaching as a whole. Many of the activities already described in this book have strong links with other areas of the curriculum. Exploring the science in baking links technology and science, exploring forces through art links art and science, exploring Victorian toys links history and science, exploring vehicles travelling down a ramp links mathematics and science, exploring musical instruments links music and science, and exploring the local environment links geography and science. Spoken and written language development occurs throughout, and literature appreciation can occur through literature-based themes. This makes science a good vehicle for cross-curricular development and enables science to be seen in a variety of everyday contexts. The concerns about cross-curricular teaching are that science can be minimalized and development limited. This is a valid argument and one used to argue against cross-curricular teaching in all curriculum areas. However, it is also an argument which can be directed at any method of delivery, and can be overcome by thorough planning and the identification of clear

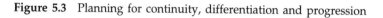

Figure 5.3 Planning for continuity, differentiation and progression

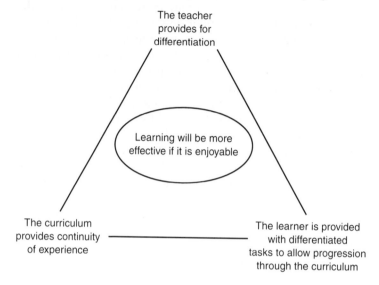

educational objectives. Careful planning is necessary to ensure that teaching provides for continuity, differentiation and progression (Figure 5.3).

Continuity, differentiation and progression are three closely linked areas which affect teaching and learning. Each has an important part to play in effective child development. Together they illustrate how effective teaching and learning are a result of the close partnership between parents, teachers, school and child. Teachers should strive to achieve continuity, differentiation and progression. However, it is also important that continuity, differentiation and progression do not become straitjackets which hinder the provision of good motivating science explorations in which children can differentiate their experiences to meet their own needs and abilities. Reality is often removed to a greater or lesser extent from the ideal and we must be realistic in our expectations, and not despair if our desired aims seem far removed from the reality in the classroom. We have already discussed the importance of continuity within the school. Continuity is the responsibility of the whole school. Shared philosophy, ideas and planning will help to provide continuity of experience. If we plan children's school experiences carefully we can ensure that they begin by learning within a familiar context and as they develop, the context becomes more unfamiliar and they have the opportunity to consider how useful their ideas are in a variety of situations. This assists their learning by firming up their ideas. Primary schools have the advantage of better liaison between Key Stages 1 and 2, usually because of day-to-day contact, and children are often unaware that they are moving between key stages. In separate infant and junior schools there needs to be good liaison to ensure that the children's development is not discontinuous. Good liaison will enable young children's exploratory work to be built upon throughout their primary school experiences. This can be and is a reality in many schools where 'family planning' takes on a different meaning and a family of schools – that is, secondary schools and their feeder primary schools – work together in curriculum areas to ensure some degree of continuity.

Classroom teachers are responsible for ensuring that the work they provide matches the needs and abilities of each child. As children are unique, with individual abilities, their educational needs will differ. The teacher will need to provide differentiated activities to meet these differing educational needs. The children's differentiated needs and abilities can be ascertained in a variety of ways (see Figure 5.1) which can involve teachers, parents and the child. Parents can provide valuable information about their children. Previous teachers can provide accurate assessments and information about the context of previous work. Children know their own abilities and will add to a developing profile of themselves. The teacher's role is to collate this information and use it to plan experiences for children which will further their scientific development.

The resulting explorations can be differentiated in a number of ways: by task; by outcome; by starting points; and by context. This can be shown through explorations on the theme of sound for Key Stage 1 children. All activities have the same learning aim in terms of the development of the concept of sound. All involve developing knowledge that there are different types of sound and sound sources, that sounds travel from the sound sources to the ear, that some sounds are fainter than others and that when further away from the source, sounds are fainter (Department for Education, 1995a). The children are given a range of objects which make sound in different ways. These can include musical instruments, toys which make a noise, a stop clock, a cassette player with cassette, a ruler, some beads in a jar and some rubber bands.

In explorations which are differentiated by outcome the children are given the objects to explore and after a period of exploration they are asked questions to find out their ideas about sounds and to help them to raise questions for further exploration. Teachers' questions can include:

- What do you notice about these objects?
- What do they all do?
- Do they make noises in different ways?
- Which ones are the noisiest/quietest?
- How do you know they are noisy or quiet?
- How can we make this sound quieter/louder?
- How can we hear the sound better?

Individual children will work at their own level and will achieve differentiated learning outcomes according to their ability. This is possibly the most common type of differentiation in the classroom. Children embark on identical tasks, but the outcome of the task will depend on the individual child. With this type of differentiation some children may never successfully complete tasks. They may experience a perpetual sense of failure, unless the task is carefully planned to enable all the children to achieve and therefore to experience a sense of success. Care needs to be taken in planning activities with a number of steps to ensure that all children will achieve a successful outcome.

Explorations on sound which are differentiated by task can take a variety of forms. They are particularly useful in a class with very wide and varying needs and abilities, for example in a vertically grouped class or where some children have special educational needs. Again children are given a range of objects which make sound in different ways. Younger or less able children can be encouraged to explore the objects and then play a sound identification game. This could be in the form of a game in which different sounds have to be described. A child or adult describes or imitates the sound and the children have to guess which object made the sound. Another game could use homemade sound lotto cards with pictures of the objects which are covered when the child hears the noise they make. The winner of the game is the first person to cover all the sounds on their card. Older or more able children could explore the sounds, and place them in order of the things that make loud sounds graduating to the things which make soft sounds. They can then draw pictures of the objects which make the loudest sounds and the objects which make the softest sounds. Even older or more able children could explore how to make a loud sound soft or a soft sound loud and draw annotated pictures of how the sound reaches their ears and why it is loud or soft. Differentiation by task also involves considerable teacher planning and organization. Special care is needed in planning and implementation to ensure that children do not feel that their work is of less importance or interest than that of others.

Activities on sound which have differentiated starting points could provide a sequence of explorations of varying difficulty. Children could work through these from different starting points, depending on their needs and abilities. This type of differentiation can have many similarities with differentiation by task, with children moving from the set activity to the next if appropriate. Children who start by exploring sounds and playing identification games could move on to sound sorting, and children beginning with explorations and sorting sounds could move on to exploring how to make sounds softer or louder. Children who begin by exploring how to make a loud sound soft or a soft sound loud could then map out quiet and loud places in the school and undertake some problem-solving to discover where the best place to undertake a loud activity would be. This type of differentiation needs care to avoid starting the child at an inappropriate level and then having to change course.

Differentiation by context takes into account that changes in context from familiar to unfamiliar make the exploration more difficult. Looking at sound within the context of music would be familiar to most children. It could take into consideration favourite music or music of different cultures and use familiar instruments to explore sounds. A more complex context would be looking at sound-proofing, although here there could be familiar or unfamiliar contexts. An exploration which looks at what material makes the best earmuffs for working in a noisy classroom is easier than one which looks at how to sound-proof a noisy clock. The context can be made more difficult by changing the questions you ask the children while they are exploring.

- Which are the quietest earmuffs?
- Which material will make the best earmuffs?
- How can you find out which material will make the best earmuffs?
- Can you find out which material will make earmuffs which are warm and sound-proof?

Thorough planning is also necessary to provide work that will allow children to progress at their own rate. Teachers can plan differentiated activities, within their schemes of work, that allow the children to progress at a rate compatible with their individual needs and abilities. This means that teachers need to plan for flexibility and the children need to be active partners in their own development. Progression in learning involves children in developing their own ideas. They need to be able to explore these and construct their own meanings, and this involves an element of flexibility in teaching. Planning is still important but planning should not be so rigid that it hinders progression.

Planning also needs to take into consideration that sequential learning is dependent upon earlier ideas and that learning may involve regression. As the work of the Science Processes and Concept Exploration (SPACE) 1986–90 and Children's Learning in Science (CLIS) 1982–9 projects indicates, there is no single way of developing ideas, and children's learning may not be linear. Indeed, it may seem on occasions that children's ideas have regressed when in fact they are more complex ideas. Progressive work should provide greater levels of demand and complexity. It should also aim to meet more complex learning objectives and involve the children in the application of previously acquired ideas, as well as new development or modifications. It is important to note that progression is different from sequencing. A teacher will provide a sequence of activities but individual children will progress through the sequence at their own rate and in their own way. The rate and way of learning are affected by many factors which cannot all be accounted for. Home life, peers, teachers, the type of work set are among factors that can all affect motivation, interest and progression.

Remember that continuity, differentiation and progression cannot be completely prescribed and the most important consideration for teachers is to do your best, relax and enjoy your teaching experiences.

Planning for organization

There are a number of different ways we can organize science in the classroom. All can be effective methods, but planning is needed to ensure that the method best matches the learning aims and objectives, and that children have the opportunity to develop scientific skills along with concepts, knowledge and attitudes. With each method of organization the teacher's role will be different. Harlen and Jelly (1989: 37) identify three roles the teacher can adopt: 'provider of expert knowledge, fellow enquirer and technician'. Changing the teaching role is a useful strategy to help children to engage in different roles within science activities.

A study of science in the National Curriculum (SCAA, 1994c) identified the most common method of organization at Key Stage 1 as small-group work with some whole-class teaching. This would be consistent with carpet-time introduction, stimulus and follow-up work and small-group explorations, which can be organized in different ways. Whole-class work can be appropriate for introducing activities, assisting organization, gathering ideas and making sense of ideas. It can also be appropriate for some activities which would be organizationally difficult in small groups, where the children's safety would be difficult to manage and where resource implications make small-group or individual work a problem. I have used whole-class time to introduce animals into the classroom. This can include pets such as rabbits, guinea-pigs, rats, mice and dogs, as well as more unusual animals such as lizards, frogs, snakes and stick insects. The animals can be introduced and emphasis can be placed on the need to be quiet and not to startle or over-handle the animals.

Other introductions and close observations could also take on a similar format. Close observation of a candle flame would be unsafe without careful adult supervision, and while whole-class carpet time would not achieve the same individual observations it would be preferable to no observations at all. Sharing observations in a large group can be beneficial in its own way, as children will have the opportunity to perceive the object from the viewpoints of others. Carpet time can also be used to share ideas after observations and explorations. They can provide the stimulus for new exploratory avenues or help children to make sense of their ideas and interpretations. The teacher's role in these sessions changes from motivator to imparter of knowledge to facilitator of learning, depending on the purpose of the activity and the teacher's interactions within the activity. While whole-class teaching is desirable for some aspects of teaching, it does have its problems. The major problem arises because it is impossible to differentiate an activity for whole-class teaching and teaching tends to be planned with the average child in mind (Alexander *et al.*, 1992).

Small-group work can take a number of different organizational forms. Groups can be organized according to ability, and this would be particularly appropriate with a class of vertically grouped children differentiated by task. It should be remembered that children's abilities in science may not be the same as their abilities in other subjects, and grouping by ability should not be taken to mean grouping by age. Crossley (1991) identified the need to group children in her class according to their level of understanding in science; Howe (1990), on the other hand, grouped children together because of their diverse ideas, and this appeared to promote their scientific understanding. Young children develop at a great rate and their abilities at Key Stage 1 can appear to be very diverse. We often assign them to ability groups based on their maturation, but we must be aware that they can mature rapidly. Ability groupings at Key Stage 1 should consider the rapid development at this age and not be rigid. Mixed-ability groups, gender groups and friendship groups can all be appropriate in different ways. Mixed-ability groups enable the less able to be supported by the more able (Jarvis, 1991). Research evidence (Smail, 1984; Assessment of Performance Unit, 1988) has indicated gender differences in abilities of primary-aged children and highlighted the merits of mixed and single-sexed groupings in science. Friendship groups can help motivate children and encourage development, although they can lead to distraction. There is no single 'correct' way to group children. I would suggest that groups are reviewed and changed regularly, so that children become used to working in a variety of situations and with different people. This would be good preparation for future life and aid the development of important group-work skills.

Within the classroom, group work can also be organized in different ways. Rotational group work is common, with children in small groups working on similar tasks throughout the day or the week. The advantage of this type of group work is that it is relatively easy to plan and easy on resources. Monitoring explorations and facilitating learning is easier if only one group of children is engaged in practical activity of this nature. Facilitating the learning becomes more difficult if there are a number of very practical activities occurring in the classroom at the same time. The role of the teacher during the group work is to question and encourage the children to follow lines of enquiry and to monitor their learning and assess their future needs. This group work could, however, be developmental, with each group taking its starting point from the previous group's end point (see Chapter 2). This type of group organization could be very appropriate for ability groups where the children differentiate the activity for the next group according to their outcome and the activity becomes more complex. When the whole class is undertaking science in small groups, it is very demanding on resources, teacher time and sanity, and I have rarely managed it effectively with Key Stage 1 children. A circus of group activities can be more successful but is equally time-consuming for the teacher. In this method of organization there are a number of differing science activities, connected to a theme. These are usually structured although they can include some exploratory activities. The activities are set out in the classroom and the children visit each activity during the course of a day or week, being briefed by the teacher at the beginning of each session. I have used this method of organization with Key Stage 2 children where one day per week has been set aside for science work. Within one year group, a science circus has enabled staff to pool expertise and resources and the children to focus on one science activity each week. This is felt (Harlen, 1985) to be of motivational advantage and be relatively easy to organize. I am not convinced about the ease of organization but agree that the main disadvantages of circus activities are the lack of coherence and continuity in the activities and the difficulties of introducing and discussing activities. The 'carpet time' becomes unmanageable.

Individual science work is usually more appropriate for older children, in that it is difficult to organize with young children. However, it can be incorporated into the early years classroom. The use of an interactive science display, science table or play area is one way to encourage individual exploration. This can take the form of a set of resources set out in the classroom which the children can interact with. There may be some simple questions or problems to solve. It may include a 'broken' electrical circuit which the children have to 'mend' or a collection of toys which move in different ways, or a collection of artefacts for close observation, drawing or printing purposes. Books and pictures can be added to encourage the children to look at secondary sources and to motivate them further within the theme. Children like to add to these collections, bringing books and artefacts from home, and this can be a good motivating link with home. I once had a collection of bones in the classroom which were added to by a small boy carrying a plastic bag with a cow's skull inside. 'I found this in a field', he said. 'I thought you would like it.' A kindly mother and a baby bath of bleach soon had the skull presentable for classroom use and it has provided many a stimulus over the years. I have also used ideas from the *Northamptonshire Science Resources Activities Box* (Creary, 1990) to provide activities related to a theme. During a topic on sound a science box was provided with plastic wallets containing ideas for explorations and a simple question. For example, one wallet contained a shaker and the instruction 'Make a sound pattern with the shaker'; it then asked 'Can you think of a way of writing down your pattern?' and gave some examples. Another contained a comb and some greaseproof paper and asked the children to make a noise with them.

Using the science table or box idea can be part of the normal Key Stage 1 day. Children could choose or be directed to the science activities as part of their structured play activities. I have found this to be a good way of motivating the children; it has led to further group and individual work arising from their own interests.

The different methods of organizing science in the classroom are all appropriate for the Key Stage 1 classroom, but not in isolation. A variety of organizational approaches is desirable as this will help to widen children's learning preferences and enhance their development.

A questioning approach in action

Planning for the teacher's role, the children's learning, for the context of learning and classroom organization seems like an enormous job. It is a task that we do almost unconsciously. The danger with 'getting on with the job' is that we do not have time to reflect on our practice and assess the children's development, with all the factors affecting it in mind. If we are able to reflect on our practice and ascertain the children's development we should be better informed to make planning decisions, for both our teaching strategies and the children's learning. We will consider an exploratory activity from both the teaching and learning viewpoints and see how they develop in practice.

Sarah had a class of 24 reception and Year 1 children. She planned a topic on minibeasts in conjunction with her school's planning and the requirements of the National Curriculum in science. She identified the main areas of learning she wished the children to develop within Attainment Target 2, Life Processes and Living Things, and Attainment Target 1, Experimental and Investigative Science. She hoped to develop the following aspects.

(a) Concepts
Variation and classification
Living things in their environment

(b) Knowledge
Minibeasts live in the local environment
Minibeasts can be found in the soil, above the soil, in the air, in plants and trees
There are different minibeasts which can be grouped according to observable features
Minibeasts are adapted to their environment
Minibeasts have needs and we should care for them

(c) Skills
Planning safe collection and study of minibeasts
Observation of minibeasts in their natural environment
Safe collection of minibeasts
Observation of minibeasts in the classroom
Raising questions about minibeasts

(d) Attitudes
Curiosity about the environment
Care for living things.

She particularly wanted to develop her teaching strategies to encourage the children to raise questions. She began to plan activities for the theme which matched her learning aims. The children had undertaken no previous work in this area, but she built into her planning opportunities for them to explore from their own interests using previous knowledge. She considered how she could develop the whole learning environment to encourage children to raise questions. One child's parent kept an allotment and grew vegetables, and the child appeared more knowledgeable about animals in the soil. This parent volunteered to come to school and help during the collection of minibeasts. Sarah collected resources which might be useful for collecting and observing minibeasts (pots, jars, pooters – small pots for collecting insects by sucking them in using two separate tubes, and which allow them to be released afterwards – paintbrushes, spades, trowels, an umbrella and magnifiers). She set up a table in the classroom with books on minibeasts, pictures and the resources for collecting and caring for them.

The introductory activity involved a carpet-time discussion where children were asked to identify any animals they might find in the school garden, field or local environment. Sarah attempted to encourage the children's ideas by allowing each child the opportunity of participating and encouraging the others to listen. She did this by using a 'gardener's hat' which had to be worn before contribution to the discussion. The children were asked to listen attentively to the person with the 'gardener's hat' on and not to speak out of turn. This was followed by discussion on how minibeasts could be carefully found and collected and the places they would most likely be found in. The children were then put into groups and each group had the responsibility of observing a different area. Each group had an adult helper, a nursery nurse and two parents, in addition to the teacher. One group looked for minibeasts in a tree, looking first at the leaves, branches and bark and then using the umbrella to hook over a branch and shake any living things out into the umbrella. Another group looked for minibeasts in the long grass at the edge of the school grounds, while a third group looked at the surface of the soil and a fourth group dug a hole about 20 centimetres into the soil and collected minibeasts from there. All groups were encouraged to note where the minibeasts were found and where possible to observe them before safely collecting them. Some minibeasts were observed in the environment and left, such as a spider in its web on the hedge at the edge of the school field.

In the classroom, the minibeasts were carefully observed, compared and grouped. The children had collected a number of minibeasts including woodlice, snails, earthworms, a beetle, a centipede, greenfly and a hairy caterpillar, as well as evidence of minibeast activity such as eaten leaves and leaf-miner tunnels. Close observation led to drawing, writing, classification using their own criteria (number of legs, shape, where found) and questions being raised about the minibeasts. At the end of the day most of the minibeasts were returned safely to their environment. The earthworms were put into a large plastic sweet jar with layers of damp compost and sand inside and leaf mould was collected and put on the top. The jar was covered with black paper and left on the display table. The woodlice were put into a plastic tub containing damp soil, some leaf mould and some pieces of rotting wood, and the caterpillar was put into a clear container with an assortment of leaves. These were put on the display table along with the books, pictures and resources. The minibeasts were kept in the classroom for a few weeks and observed and cared for by the children. As Sarah wanted to develop the children's ability to raise questions, she used a variety of strategies to encourage this development. She planned questions to focus their observations and develop their questioning skills. For example, she asked each group of children to note all their observations and to share them with the rest of the class during carpet time. During the class discussions she used a white-board to record the questions raised, and she used some of these questions to make question cards to put on the display with the minibeasts.

- Where does it live?
- How many legs?
- What can you see?
- What does it eat?

She then asked the children to identify which questions they could begin to answer from their observations. The children used their observations to keep individual records of the minibeasts and tried to answer the questions. Leanne chose to keep a record of the caterpillar. She was interested in the caterpillar's food, having been motivated by the story of *The Very Hungry Caterpillar* (Carle, 1970). The caterpillar ate a great deal of leaves, although not lollipops, Swiss cheese and ice cream, and then stopped eating.

Table 5.3   Roles and experience in a topic on minibeasts

Teacher's role	Children's experience
Researcher and planner	
Motivator	Whole-class introduction to topic
Instructor	Whole-class instruction in collecting and caring for minibeasts
Guide	Group observation and collection of minibeasts
Interactor	Small-group observations and question raising
Convener	Small-group and whole-class discussions
Motivator	Adding to interactive display
Guide and interactor	Small-group and individual recording of minibeasts

Leanne predicted that the caterpillar would turn into a butterfly quickly, but it seemed to take a long time. She was puzzled but kept watching. When the minibeast topic was complete and the other minibeasts returned to their natural environment, the chrysalis was kept in the classroom and Leanne, along with other children, kept a close watch on it. When it eventually turned into a moth, Leanne was delighted and finished the last page of her 'caterpillar diary'. An extended study had resulted from a small hairy caterpillar found in the school grounds. The moth was released into the playground and the children watched it fly away.

During this work there were a number of different teaching roles and learning experiences. These are listed in Table 5.3. During the teaching and learning, Sarah observed the children and made assessments of their learning in line with her main learning aims. In some cases she adjusted teaching and learning demands according to the needs of individual children. One group of reception children found group interaction difficult. Sarah gave each child the task of observing and writing about one minibeast and compiling a group book about the minibeasts. The children had to decide which minibeast they wished to observe and plan their book before they could work individually. They needed help in putting the book together, but they made some attempt at developing group-work skills.

After each stage of the teaching it was necessary for Sarah to

reflect on her teaching and the children's learning and to be flexible enough to modify her planning to meet her learning aims, or
modify her learning aims to meet the needs of the children. Good
planning was necessary, but not inflexibility.

I hope that all teachers would have not only the ability, but
also a willingness, to reflect on their own practice. Teacher education, both initial training and in-service, should involve elements
of classroom action research. Classroom action research on initial
teacher training courses is felt to be extremely valuable by both
students and educationists (Elliott, 1991), and I see student
teachers entering the teaching profession having researched
children's learning and their own practice, and with a clear idea
of their teaching role. The skills developed as a result benefit
both the children's learning and the teaching strategies to aid
that learning.

Summary

The teacher's role is varied and complex. Teachers need to plan
carefully not only for the children's learning but for their own
role to facilitate that learning. Effective teachers of young children are also reflective teachers. They are able to plan collaboratively for children's scientific development, find out children's
previous knowledge and skills and take on a variety of teaching
roles to facilitate that learning. For young children the most effective roles involve the teacher as a facilitator of learning rather than
an imparter of knowledge. The roles most used in Key Stage 1
classrooms are the teacher as a

- motivator
- guide
- instructor
- interactor
- convener
- assessor
- evaluator.

These roles need to be planned to provide effective teaching and
learning.

Developments in primary science, both before and since the
introduction of the National Curriculum, have been rapid and

extensive. All young children have scientific opportunities at primary school, and their science experiences are becoming more interesting and relevant. As teachers have become more experienced, they have also become more motivated and enthusiastic. The greatest justification for effective primary science teaching and learning is the enthusiasm, interest and understanding of the children themselves. In many cases it is the children who motivate the teachers and help to develop their confidence and enthusiasm. The increased confidence, enthusiasm and understanding of teachers in turn lead to the provision of more exploratory science experiences which are best suited to effective learning.

Useful reading

Association for Science Education (1988) *Initiatives in Primary Science: An Evaluation. Building Bridges – Towards Continuity and Progression.* Hatfield: ASE.

Galton, M. and Harlen, W. (1990) *Assessing Science in the Primary Classroom* (series). London: Paul Chapman.

Harrison, S. and Theaker, K. (1989) *Curriculum Leadership and Co-ordination in the Primary School. A Handbook for Teachers.* Whalley: Guild House Press.

Kilshaw, M. (1990) Using concept maps. *Primary Science Review,* 12: 34–6.

National Curriculum Council (1993) *Teaching Science at Key Stages 1 and 2.* York: NCC.

Osborne, J. (1990) *Light,* Primary Science Processes and Concept Exploration (SPACE) project research report. Liverpool: Liverpool University Press.

Osborne, J. (1991) *Electricity,* Primary Science Processes and Concept Exploration (SPACE) research report. Liverpool: Liverpool University Press.

Osborne, J. (1994) *Earth in Space,* Primary Science Processes and Concept Exploration (SPACE) project research report. Liverpool: Liverpool University Press.

Russell, T. (1993) *Soil and Weather,* Primary Science Processes and Concept Exploration (SPACE) project research report. Liverpool: Liverpool University Press.

Russell, T. and Watt, D. (1990) *Evaporation and Condensation,* Primary Science Processes and Concept Exploration (SPACE) project research report. Liverpool: Liverpool University Press.

Russell, T. and Watt, D. (1990) *Growth*, Primary Science Processes and Concept Exploration (SPACE) project research report. Liverpool: Liverpool University Press.

Russell, T., Langden, K. and McGuigan, L. (1991) *Materials*, Primary Science Processes and Concept Exploration (SPACE) project research report. Liverpool: Liverpool University Press.

Schön, D. (1983) *The Reflective Practitioner*. New York: Basic Books.

Schön, D. (1987) *Educating the Reflective Practitioner*. San Francisco: Jossey-Bass.

School Curriculum and Assessment Authority (1995) *Planning the Curriculum at Key Stages 1 and 2*. London: SCAA.

Scott, P. (1987) *A Constructivist View of Learning and Teaching in Science. Children's Learning in Science Project*. Leeds: Centre for Research in Primary Science and Technology.

Watt, D. and Russell, T. (1990) *Sound*, Primary Science Processes and Concept Exploration (SPACE) project research report. Liverpool: Liverpool University Press.

References

Ahlberg, A. (1981) *Mrs Lather's Laundry*. London: Penguin (Picture Puffin).

Ahlberg, J. and Ahlberg, A. (1980) *Funnybones*. London: Collins Picture Lions.

Alexander, R., Rose, J. and Woodhead, C. (1992) *Curriculum Organisation and Classroom Practice in Primary Schools: A Discussion Paper*. London: Department of Education and Science.

Antonouris, G. (1991) Teaching science in a multicultural society. *Primary Science Review*, 17: 3–7.

Assessment of Performance Unit (1988) *Science at Age 11. A Review of APU Survey Findings 1980–84*. London: HMSO.

Association for Science Education (1993) *The Whole Curriculum in Primary Schools – Maintaining Quality in the Teaching of Primary Science*. Hatfield: ASE.

Association for Science Education (1994) *The Association Conference, Nottingham 1994*. Hatfield: ASE.

Association for Science Education, Association of Teachers of Mathematics, Mathematical Association and National Association for the Teaching of English (1989) *The National Curriculum – Making It Work for the Primary School*. Hatfield: ASE.

Ausubel, D. (1968) *Educational Psychology: A Cognitive View*. New York: Holt, Rinehart & Winston.

Barnes, D. (1976) *From Communication to Curriculum*. Harmondsworth: Penguin.

Bowell, B., France, S. and Redfern, S. (1994) *Portable Computers in Action*. Coventry: National Council for Educational Technology.

Briggs, R. (1970) *Jim and the Beanstalk*. London: Penguin (Picture Puffin).

Carle, E. (1970) *The Very Hungry Caterpillar*. Harmondsworth: Penguin.

Catsambis, S. (1995) Gender, race, ethnicity and science education in the middle grades. *Journal of Research in Science Teaching*, 32: 243–57.

Cavendish, S., Galton, M., Hargreaves, L. and Harlen, W. (1990) *Observing Activities*. Assessing Science in the Primary Classroom series. London: Paul Chapman.

Chambers, D.W. (1983) Stereotypic images of the scientist. *Science Education*, 62: 225–65.

Chapman, B. (1991) The overselling of science in the eighties. *Schools Science Review*, 72(26): 47–63.

Chemical Industries Association (1994) Schools Education: Position Statement. Unpublished.

Childs, D. (1986) *Psychology and the Teacher*, 4th edn. Chatham: Holt, Rinehart & Winston.

Cosgrove, M. and Osborne, R. (1985) Lesson frameworks for changing children's ideas. In R. Osborne and P. Freyberg, *Learning in Science: The Implications of Children's Learning*. Auckland, New Zealand: Heinemann.

Council for the Accreditation of Teacher Education (1993) *The Initial Teaching of Primary Teachers: Circular 14/93 (England)*. London: CATE.

Creary, C. (1990) *Northamptonshire Science Resources Activities Box: Resources for Key Stage 1*. Northampton: Northamptonshire County Council.

Cross, A. (1992) Pictorial concept maps – putting us in the picture. *Primary Science Review*, 21: 26–8.

Crossley, J. (1991) Grouping for science. *Primary Science Review*, 17: 8–9.

Cumming, J. (1995) An Easter science and technology project involving parents. *Primary Science Review*, 36: 4–7.

Cunliffe, J. (1987) *Postman Pat's Summer Storybook*. London: André Deutsch.

Dearing, R. (1993) *The National Curriculum and Its Assessment: Final Report*. London: School Curriculum and Assessment Authority.

Department for Education (1993) *Circular 14/93: The Initial Training of Primary School Teachers*. London: HMSO.

Department for Education (1995a) *Science in the National Curriculum*. London: HMSO.

Department for Education (1995b) *Information Technology in the National Curriculum*. London: HMSO.

Department of Education and Science (1985) *The Curriculum from 5 to 16. Curriculum Matters 2*. London: HMSO.

Department of Education and Science (1987) *National Curriculum Science Working Group. Interim Report*. London: DES.

Department of Education and Science (1988) *A Report: National Task Group on Assessment and Testing*. London: DES.

Department of Education and Science (1989) *The Education Reform Act 1988: National Curriculum: Mathematics and Science Orders under Section 4. Circular 6/89*. London: HMSO.

Department of Education and Science (1991a) *The Education Reform Act 1988: National Curriculum: Mathematics and Science Orders under Section 4. Circular 17/91*. London: HMSO.

Department of Education and Science (1991b) *Science Key Stages 1 and 3: The Implementation of the Curricular Requirements of the Education Reform Act. A Report by HM Inspectorate on the First Year, 1989–90*. London: HMSO.

Donaldson, M. (1978) *Children's Minds*. London: Fontana.

Driver, R. (1983) *The Pupil as a Scientist*. Milton Keynes: Open University Press.

Driver, R., Guesne, E. and Tiberghien, A. (eds) (1985) *Children's Ideas in Science*. Milton Keynes: Open University Press.

Eland, S., Jackson, P., Johnston, J. and Snow, N. (1995a) *Let's Investigate Forces*. Nottingham: Nottingham Trent University.

Eland, S., Jackson, P., Johnston, J. and Snow, N. (1995b) *Let's Investigate Light*. Nottingham: Nottingham Trent University.

Eland, S., Jackson, P., Johnston, J. and Snow, N. (1995c) *Let's Investigate Materials*. Nottingham: Nottingham Trent University.

Eland, S., Jackson, P., Johnston, J. and Snow, N. (1995d) *Let's Investigate Electricity*. Nottingham: Nottingham Trent University.

Eland, S., Jackson, P., Johnston, J. and Snow, N. (1995e) *Let's Investigate Energy*. Nottingham: Nottingham Trent University.

Elliott, J. (1991) *Action Research for Educational Change*. Milton Keynes: Open University Press.

Elstgeest, J., Harlen, W. and Symington, D. (1985) Children communicate. In W. Harlen (ed.), *Primary Science: Taking the Plunge*. London: Heinemann.

Erikson, G.L. (1979) Children's conceptions of heat and temperature. *Science Education*, 63: 221–30.

Faire, J. and Cosgrove, M. (1988) *Teaching Primary Science*. Hamilton, New Zealand: Waikato Education Centre.

Fleer, M. (1993) Pedagogical developments in early childhood and primary science teaching. In D. Goodrum (ed.), *Science in the Early Years of Schooling: An Australian Perspective*. Perth, WA: National Key Centre for School Science and Mathematics, Curtin University of Technology.

Fraser, B. and Tobin, K. (1993) Exemplary science and mathematics teachers. In B. Fraser (ed.), *Research Implications for Science and Mathematics Teachers, Volume 1*. Perth, WA: National Key Centre for School Science and Mathematics, Curtin University of Technology.

Gold, K. (1990) Get thee to a laboratory. *New Scientist*, 126(1712): 42–6.

Goldsworthy, A. (1989) Observation under observation. *Primary Science Review*, 9: 24–6.

Goldsworthy, A. and Feasey, R. (1994) *Making Sense of Primary Investigations*. Hatfield: Association for Science Education.

Harlen, W. (ed.) (1977a) *Match and Mismatch: Raising Questions*. Edinburgh: Oliver & Boyd.

Harlen, W. (ed.) (1977b) *Match and Mismatch: Finding Answers*. Edinburgh: Oliver & Boyd.

Harlen, W. (1985) *Teaching and Learning Primary Science*. London: Paul Chapman.

Harlen, W. (1992) *The Teaching of Science: Studies in Primary Education*. London: David Fulton.

Harlen, W. (1993) Moving the goalposts. *Primary Science Review*, 28: 2–3.

Harlen, W. and Jelly, S. (1989) *Developing Science in the Primary Classroom*. Harlow: Oliver & Boyd.

Harlen, W. and Symington, D. (1985) Helping children to observe. In W. Harlen (ed.), *Primary Science: Taking the Plunge*. London: Heinemann.

Hayes, M. and Johnston, J. (1993) Study visit to Finland to investigate how teachers view science and the teaching of information technology and science. Unpublished report to the Central Bureau for Educational Visits and Exchanges, Nottingham Trent University.

Hayes, M. and Johnston, J. (1995) The importance of science perceptions in the development of science. Paper presented to the conference on Science Education Research in Europe.

Hill, E. (1984) *Spot's Toys*. London: Heinemann.

Howe, C. (1990) Grouping children for effective learning in science. *Primary Science Review*, 13: 26–7.

Jackson, P. (1993a) After the goldrush. *Strategies*, 3(3): 14–19.

Jackson, P. (1993b) The Wakatipu kite festival. *Strategies*, 3(5): 23–6.

Jarvis, T. (1991) *Children and Primary Science*. London: Cassell.

Jarvis, T. (1994) Schools-based tasks in science for primary postgraduate initial teacher trainees. Paper presented to the Conference for the Australian Science Teachers Association (CONASTA) conference.

Jelly, S. (1985) Helping children raise questions – and answering them. In W. Harlen (ed.), *Primary Science: Taking the Plunge*. London: Heinemann.

Johnston, J. (1992) The science straitjacket. *Primary Science Review*, 25: 8–9.

Johnston, J. (1995) The gap between the public perception of science and realities of science. Paper presented to the conference of the National Association for Research in Science Teaching.

Karplus, R. (1977) *Science Teaching and the Development of Reasoning.* Berkeley, CA: University of California Press.

King, C. (1963) *Stig of the Dump.* Harmondsworth: Penguin.

Lewis, M. (1992) Investigating ice balloons. *Primary Science Review*, 21: 12–13.

May, S. (1985) *Planet of the Monsters.* London: Picture Corgi.

McClelland, G. (1983) Ausubel's theory of meaningful learning and its implications for primary science. In C. Richards and D. Holford (eds) *The Teaching of Primary Science: Policy and Practice.* Lewes: Falmer Press.

Medawar, P.B. (1969) *Induction and Intuition in Scientific Thought. Memoirs of the American Philosophical Society. Jayne Lectures 1968.* London: Methuen.

Millar, R. and Wynne, B. (1988) Public understanding of science. *International Journal of Science Education*, 10: 388–98.

Munn, N. (1966) *Psychology*, 5th edn. London: Harrap.

National Board of Employment, Education and Training (1993) *What Do They Know? The Understanding of Science and Technology by Children in Their Last Year of Primary School in Australia. Commissioned Report No. 23.* Canberra: Australian Government Printing Service.

National Curriculum Council (1989) *Science: Non-statutory Guidance.* York: NCC.

National Curriculum Council (1990) *Curriculum Guidance 4: Economic and Industrial Understanding.* York: NCC.

Novak, J. and Gowan, D.B. (1984) *Learning How to Learn.* Cambridge: Cambridge University Press.

Osborne, R. and Freyberg, P. (1985) *Learning in Science: The Implications of Children's Learning.* Auckland, New Zealand: Heinemann.

Osborne, J., Wadsworth, P. and Black, P. (1992) *Materials*, Primary Science Processes and Concept Exploration (SPACE) project research report. Liverpool: Liverpool University Press.

Ovens, P. (1987) Ice balloons. *Primary Science Review*, 3: 5–6.

Piaget, J. (1929) *The Child's Conception of the World.* New York: Harcourt.

Piaget, J. (1950) *The Psychology of Intelligence.* London: Routledge & Kegan Paul.

Raper, G. and Stringer, J. (1987) *Encouraging Primary Science.* London: Cassell.

Reiss, M.J. (1993) *Science Education for a Pluralist Society. Developing Science and Technology Education.* Buckingham: Open University Press.

Renner, J. (1982) The power of purpose. *Science Education*, 66: 709–16.

Richards, C. (ed.) (1984) *The Study of Primary Education: A Source Book. Volume 1.* London: Falmer Press.

Rogers, S. (1993) 'A study to improve my strategies for teaching a mixed group of Year 4 children in order to develop positive attitudes to science', unpublished BEd study. Nottingham Trent University.

Rowland, R. (1981) How to intervene: clues from the work of a ten year old. *Forum*, 23(2): 33–5.

Rowland, R. (1984) *The Enquiring Classroom: an Approach to Understanding Children's Learning*. London: Falmer Press.

School Curriculum and Assessment Authority (1994a) *Evaluation of the Implementation of Science in the National Curriculum at Key Stages 1, 2 and 3. Volume 1: Executive Summary and Coverage. Research for the National Curriculum Council by the Centre for Research in Primary Science and Technology, University of Liverpool*. London: SCAA.

School Curriculum and Assessment Authority (1994b) *Evaluation of the Implementation of Science in the National Curriculum at Key Stages 1, 2 and 3. Volume 2: Progression. Research for the National Curriculum Council by the Centre for Research in Primary Science and Technology, University of Liverpool*. London: SCAA.

School Curriculum and Assessment Authority (1994c) *Evaluation of the Implementation of Science in the National Curriculum at Key Stages 1, 2 and 3. Volume 3: Differentiation. Research for the National Curriculum Council by the Centre for Research in Primary Science and Technology, University of Liverpool*. London: SCAA.

School Curriculum and Assessment Authority (1994d) *The Review of the National Curriculum: A Report on the 1994 Consultation*. London: SCAA.

Scott, P. (1987) *A Constructivist View of Learning and Teaching in Science*. Leeds: Leeds University.

Simon, A., Jones, A., Fairbrother, R., Watson, J. and Black, P. (1992a) *Open Work in Science: A Review of Existing Practice*. London: King's College.

Simon, A., Jones, A., Fairbrother, R., Watson, J. and Black, P. (1992b) *Open Work in Science: Development of Investigations in Schools*. Hatfield: Association for Science Education.

Smail, B. (1984) *Girl-Friendly Science: Avoiding Sex Bias in the Curriculum*. York: Schools Council/Longman.

Solomon, J. and Lee, J. (1991) *School Home Investigations in Primary Science*. Hatfield: Association for Science Education.

Symington, D. (1978) Primary school pupils' ability to see investigable scientific problems in everyday phenomena: the teacher's role. *Research in Science Education*, 8: 167–74.

Vygotsky, L. (1962) *Thought and Language*. Cambridge, MA: MIT Press.

Wilde, O. (1978) *The Selfish Giant*. London: Penguin (Picture Puffin).

Woolnough, B.E. (1994) *Effective Science Teaching. Developing Science and Technology Education*. Buckingham: Open University Press.

Index

EFFECTIVE EARLY YEARS EDUCATION
TEACHING YOUNG CHILDREN

Anne Edwards and Peter Knight

In this concise and accessible guide, the authors are sympathetic to
the particular demands of teaching three to eight year olds and offer
practical solutions to the complex issues that are currently faced by
early years educators. In recognizing the demands on practitioners,
they provide new and challenging frameworks for an understanding
of the practice of teaching young children and draw upon
international research to offer a sound model of early years subject-
structured teaching which has the quality of children's learning at its
centre. Their aim is to support teaching expertise through stimulating
teachers' thinking about children's development, motivation, ways of
learning and the subjects they teach. These topics are clearly set in
the complex institutional settings in which practitioners work and
ways of taking and evaluating action are offered.

Contents
*Introduction: education from three to eight – Becoming a pupil – Children's
learning – A curriculum for the early years – Subjects and the early years
curriculum – The organization of the learning environment – Parents and
professionals – Developing the curriculum – Developing the organization –
Endpiece – References – Index.*

176pp   0 335 19188 6 (Paperback)   0 335 19189 4 (Hardback)

PRIMARY SCIENCE AND TECHNOLOGY
PRACTICAL ALTERNATIVES

Di Bentley and Mike Watts (eds)

This book explores the ways in which science and technology can take place in the early and middle years at school. At the heart of the book are a number of case studies of actual practice drawn from primary schools in action. These studies contribute to a theoretical approach grounded in children's learning, and are used in exploring the real problems of planning, management, organization, teaching and learning as classroom practitioners try to implement new curriculum directives. The chapters examine the nature of learning experiences, the practice of teaching, teaching for specific skills, the role of the specialist coordinator, assessment and record keeping, scientific and technological problem solving and working for equal opportunities. The authors draw on their own wide experience in science education and upon their work with teachers in primary classrooms.

Contents
Building on experience – Learning and conceptual change – Conceptual development and language – School planning for conceptual change – Planning for the curriculum and the classroom – Classroom organization and management – Posing problems: effective questioning – Solving problems in science and technology – Working for equal opportunities – Teacher assessment – Being a co-ordinator – Teacher knowledge and teacher education – Appendices – References – Index.

Contributors
Steve Alsop, Brenda Barber, Di Bentley, Rosemary Denman, Catherine Ducheck, Jane Eaton, B. Hodgson, Jenny McGivern, Sue Marran, P. Murphy, Cindy Palmer, Pauline Prince, Jenny Saady, E. Scanlon, Amanda Walsh, Mike Watts, Virginia Whitby, Elizabeth Whitelegg, Doreen Wootton.

240pp   0 335 19028 6 (paperback)   0 335 19029 4 (hardback)